BIRDS

OF THE SMOKIES

TEXT BY
FRED J. ALSOP, III

GREAT SMOKY MOUNTAINS
ASSOCIATION
Gatlinburg, Tennessee

EDITED BY: Steve Kemp
EDITORIAL ASSISTANCE: Lynne Davis and Don DeFoe
DESIGNED BY: Christina Watkins
ILLUSTRATED BY: Michael Taylor
PRODUCTION AND COORDINATION BY: Steve Kemp
TYPOGRAPHY BY: TypeWorks, Tucson, AZ
COVER PHOTOGRAPH BY: Jim Cammack
PRINTED IN HONG KONG

12   13   14   15

ISBN 0-937207-05-5

Great Smoky Mountains Association is a nonprofit organization
which supports the educational, scientific, and historical programs of Great Smoky Mountains National Park. Our publications are an educational service intended to enhance the pub-
lic's understanding and enjoyment of the national park. If you would
like to know more about our publications, memberships,
and projects, please contact: Great Smoky Mountains
Association, P.O. Box 130, Gatlinburg, TN
37738. Phone 865.436.7318. Or visit our website at
SmokiesInformation.org.

To my parents
Billie J. and Fred Alsop, Jr.
For a lifetime of encouragement and love,
and for maintaining their sense of humor
when their eldest son became a birdwatcher.

To all those great birders with whom I have spent
so many enjoyable hours pursuing birds
in this truly outstanding national park.

PREFACE

More than 36 years have passed since I first birded Great Smoky Mountains National Park as a student in Dr. David H. Snyder's first ornithology class at Austin Peay State University. It has been my great good fortune to have spent countless days since observing, recording, and photographing birds in the park. In the fall of 1966, I entered The University of Tennessee, Knoxville, as a graduate student in zoology and began to make regular birding trips to the Smokies. I helped lead my first bird-watching trip in the park in 1967, with James M. Campbell, as part of the annual Wildflower Pilgrimage. During the summers of 1968 and 1969 I was a seasonal ranger-naturalist in the park and compiled my first checklist of the birds of Great Smoky Mountains National Park. It was during these early days as a graduate student and a seasonal ranger that I first began to think about writing this book.

In the interim I have continued to bird in the park whenever I could. I have led field trips as part of the annual Wildflower Pilgrimage and been an instructor in the Smoky Mountain Field School. There have been thousands of marvelous hours spent watching and photographing the birds, taking field notes, and leading field trips. There has been the challenge and exhilaration of showing the park's birds to thousands of birders, from novices to pros, with more than a few life birds sprinkled in for everyone.

The primary objectives of this book are to present an accurate account of the birds of the park, to illustrate the most common and conspicuous species, and to provide information on how, when, and where to locate birds in the park. The interpretation of the records of each species' occurrence and status is strictly my own, based on my personal knowledge and experience, and on the published and unpublished records of many reliable birders. I have sought to be conservative in this approach. Therefore, I have not included in the checklist any questionable species, and have followed the rule, "when in doubt, throw it out."

Finally, I hope this book is useful to you as you seek to identify, to locate, or to learn more about the birds of Great Smoky Mountains National Park. Many years ago Arthur Stupka personalized my copy of his book on the park's birds with, "I hope this will be a slight aid in directing many of these species your way." These are my wishes for you. Good birding!

ACKNOWLEDGMENTS

I am indebted to many people for their companionship on countless birding trips and for their encouragement and assistance on the many stages that have led to the completion of this work. It is not possible to thank them all individually in this space, but I would like to single out several for special recognition:

To David H. Snyder, my undergraduate mentor, whose energies and motivation created a spark for the challenge of birding that has grown for 27 years.

To James M. Campbell, who taught me to bird with my ears in addition to my eyes, and who arranged for me to lead my first field trips with him in the Smokies.

To G. Ronald Austing, who taught me how to photograph birds, and who spent countless hours in the field and in photo blinds with me sharing decades of experience.

To my co-leaders of the annual Wildflower Pilgrimage birding field trips, and my great good friends in the field for many years: Georgann Schmalz, Marcia L. Davis, Linda Fowler, Betty Reid Campbell, and again, James M. Campbell. We've seen lots of birds together and shown them to many, many others.

To Cathi J. Sullins, Rick Pyeritz, Rick A. Phillips, and Tom F. Laughlin, for continued excitement of many birding trips in the Smokies.

To all the good folks in the Knoxville Chapter of the Tennessee Ornithological Society. We've spent many fine birding days in the Smokies on club field trips and Christmas Bird Counts during my graduate school days in Knoxville. In particular, I wish to thank James T. Tanner and Joseph C. Howell, my teachers and field companions, and Chester A. Massey.

Finally, to various personnel connected with Great Smoky Mountains National Park as naturalists and rangers, especially Don DeFoe and Dennis K. Huffman.

To my friend Lawrence G. Isaacs in grateful appreciation for his thorough proofreading of this manuscript.

To the editor Steve Kemp, whose patience and cheerful cooperation made the dream of this book become a reality.

Fred J. Alsop, III
Johnson City, Tennessee
January, 1991

CONTENTS

PREFACE vi

ACKNOWLEDGMENTS viii

INTRODUCTION 12

BIRDING IN THE PARK 19

BIRD CHECKLIST 28

THE TOPOGRAPHY OF A BIRD 34

MAP OF GREAT SMOKY MOUNTAINS
   NATIONAL PARK 36

100 BIRD SPECIES 38

THE BIRDER'S DOZEN 138

BIRD FINDING IN THE PARK 147

PHOTOGRAPHING BIRDS 161

BIRD SONGS 162

BIBLIOGRAPHY & SELECTED
   REFERENCES 165

INDEX 166

INTRODUCTION

Great Smoky Mountains National Park—what a magnificent place to look at birds. Here is a vast area of virtually unspoiled forests, broken only in a few small areas by man-made clearings in low elevation coves. Great Smoky Mountains National Park is large, at least by Eastern standards. It encompasses over 800 square miles in an area more than 54 miles from east to west and averaging more than 15 miles from north to south. It is one of the greenest places in the United States, dominated by vegetation-covered, gently contoured mountains reaching a maximum elevation of 6,643 feet on Clingmans Dome (the third highest peak in the eastern United States). The crest of the Great Smoky Mountains forms the state boundary between Tennessee and North Carolina. It bisects the park from northeast to southwest in an unbroken chain that rises more than 5,000 feet high for over 36 miles.

There is a considerable diversity of habitat, topography, and climatic conditions between Clingmans Dome and the park's lowlands. Rainfall in the lower elevations averages 55 inches annually. As you ascend the mountains to the spruce-fir forests, the annual precipitation increases to about 90 inches, making the area the second wettest place in the contiguous United States. Diversity of habitats, heavy rainfall, and a long growing season have combined to produce the development of a world-renowned variety of flora in these mist-shrouded mountains. There are nearly 100 species of native trees, more than 1,500 additional kinds of flowering plants, hundreds of species of mosses, liverworts, and lichens, and over 2,000 different fungi.

HABITATS FROM TOP TO BOTTOM . . . .

Although forested areas in the Temperate Zone are not noted for their great variety of birds, more than 230 species have been reliably recorded within the park boundaries. At least 110 of these species breed in the park and at least 61 are permanent residents.

The spruce-fir forests that crown the highest ridges reach their southernmost limit in the eastern United States just a few miles west of Clingmans Dome and provide the only clearly defined "life-zone," the Canadian zone, in the park. This dark, damp, often cloud-veiled coniferous forest is very similar to the low elevation boreal forest 1,000 miles to the north. This is the southernmost part of the breeding range for many "northern" plants and animals, including the Black-capped Chickadee, Golden-crowned Kinglet, Red-breasted Nuthatch, Northern Saw-whet Owl, Blackburnian Warbler, Canada Warbler, Veery, and Winter Wren. Chestnut-sided Warblers are common birds in the disturbed areas where blackberry tangles thrive; Blue-headed Vireos and Brown Creepers sing from the trees and the Dark-eyed Junco is abundant. Common Ravens soar playfully overhead.

The northern hardwood and the cove hardwood forests are mixing grounds for northern and southern species of birds. In these great forests a dozen "northern" or "high elevation" breeding species reach their lowest elevation limits as nesting birds and almost as many "southern" birds reach their highest altitudinal limit. You can find "northern" Black-capped Chickadees, Veerys, Blue-headed Vireos, Winter Wrens, Yellow-bellied Sapsuckers, Rose-breasted Grosbeaks, Black-throated Blue Warblers, and Dark-eyed Juncos in an overlap zone with such "southern" species as Carolina Chickadees, Wood Thrushes, Red-eyed Vireos, Carolina Wrens, Northern Cardinals, Hooded Warblers, and the Tufted Titmouse.

This densely forested area with its 100-foot tall trees can be a frustrating place to bird if you must rely entirely on sight. Birds are frequently obscured by the foliage and those species that sing and forage in the forest canopy are especially difficult to see. Species that make their living in the interior of the forest are often in dim light as much of the sunlight is filtered out before it reaches the forest floor. Then there are those birds that favor the interior of rhododendron thickets and other tangles and seem always to be phantoms on the opposite side of the clump. If you begin to learn a few of the songs of the more common species, songs that you will hear repeatedly during the breeding season, you will successfully locate more species on each birding trip. You will hear many more birds singing than you will ever see in the lush eastern deciduous and evergreen spruce-fir forests.

The southern hardwoods in the middle and lower elevations have the greatest diversity of plant and animal species as well as the greatest numbers of birds. Most of the birds encountered are the "typical" species one would expect to find in mature woodlands at similar elevations in eastern Tennessee or western North Carolina. Commonly observed species include the Downy Woodpecker, Red-bellied Woodpecker, Eastern Screech-Owl, Belted Kingfisher, Blue Jay, Carolina Chickadee, Carolina Wren, Eastern Bluebird, Northern Cardinal, Song Sparrow, and American Goldfinch. In summer add the Yellow-billed Cuckoo, Eastern Wood-Pewee, Acadian Flycatcher, Blue-gray Gnatcatcher, Wood Thrush, Yellow-throated Vireo, Red-eyed Vireo, Black-and-white Warbler, Ovenbird, Louisiana Waterthrush, Kentucky Warbler, Hooded Warbler, Scarlet Tanager, Indigo Bunting, and Chipping Sparrow. In winter, Yellow-rumped Warblers, White-throated Sparrows, and Dark-eyed Juncos become common.

The fields and pastures in such places as Cades Cove provide habitats for birds that require open areas. These locations are suited to the Turkey Vulture, Red-tailed Hawk, American Kestrel, Northern Bobwhite, Wild Turkey, Killdeer, Mourning Dove, American Crow, Eastern Bluebird, American Robin, European Starling, Field Sparrow, Red-winged Blackbird, and Eastern Meadowlark. In summer add the Eastern Kingbird, Barn Swallow, Yellow Warbler, Yellow-throated Warbler, Indigo Bunting, and Orchard Oriole. In winter look for the Common Snipe and Savannah Sparrow.

SEASONS IN THE SMOKIES . . . .

Except for the 60 or so species that are permanent residents in the park, the numbers of birds and the diversity of species change with the seasons. Temperatures begin to drop dramatically in October and November and the mountains begin to cool. As a rule, the temperature decreases an average of three degrees Fahrenheit for every 1,000-foot increase in elevation. Consequently, the average temperature for January atop a 6,000 foot mountain peak in the Great Smokies is equivalent to the temperature in Central Ohio. The average July temperature at that same elevation is duplicated along the southern edge of Hudson Bay in Canada. In winter, the fewest species of birds occur and most of these will be in the low to middle elevations. The few hardy species that stay in the snow-laden spruce-fir forests include the Common Raven, Dark-eyed Junco, Red-breasted Nuthatch, Black-capped Chickadee, and erratically fluctuating numbers of wintering Pine Siskins, Evening Grosbeaks, and Red Crossbills. Many birds migrate downslope in winter. Christmas Bird Counts under the guidelines of the National Audubon Society have been conducted annually in the park since 1935 and an average day's count will produce around 65 species.

Winter is an unpredictable season. Birds are easier to observe because the deciduous trees have dropped their leaves. However, except for their call notes, few are singing. (Carolina Wrens, Northern Cardinals, and Song Sparrows seem to sing on any warm, sunny day from late December into spring.)

Climatic conditions may change rapidly during these months. Days that begin mild and sunny may soon become cold and windy with clouds veiling the summits and icy rain or snow falling in the higher elevations. Winter and early spring can be rainy and birders should be prepared to dress for cold, windy, and wet conditions. Sometimes it is possible on such days to change the weather by just changing altitudes. Snow or rain at Newfound Gap may be traded for light, misty drizzle at Sugarlands, or for drier conditions still in Cades Cove. Move around and see if you can salvage part of a "bad" weather day (sometimes you just have to give it up for the dry indoors and the exhibits in the Sugarlands Visitor Center).

Spring can be a protracted season in the park. In January, after a few days of unseasonably mild weather and warm rains, some spring-like activities can be observed in the lower elevations. Wood frogs (*Rana sylvatica*) may congregate in wet roadside ditches and temporary pools to mate and lay eggs. The American Woodcock's nasal *peent* calls can be heard from the old fields and woodland edges in the last half hour of twilight. Great Horned Owls may select a nest site and lay their eggs. You might hear their deep hooting calls from the woodlands at dusk, during the night, and again at dawn. Mourning Doves will follow suit in February.

The lengthening days and warmer weather in March bring forth numerous wildflowers and many of the resident songbirds begin to sing more frequently and to establish territories. The second half of the month will bring the first migrating songbirds, giving a taste of the waves to follow. New arrivals include Blue-gray Gnatcatchers, Blue-headed Vireos, Black-and-white Warblers, Yellow-throated Warblers, and Louisiana Waterthrushes. In April, many more migrants and summer residents appear almost daily, and in the lower to middle elevations many species begin nesting. This is a period filled with birdsong, and until mates are attracted and territorial boundaries secured, the singing continues throughout much of the day.

Because of the great range of elevations between the low, forested valleys and the lofty summits, spring does not come to all places in the park at the same time. It is, therefore, possible to follow spring uphill and back in time as you climb upward from Gatlinburg or Cherokee to the spruce-fir forests on Newfound Gap or Clingmans Dome. In late April, hundreds of wildflowers may be blooming in the lower to middle elevations and many species of birds may be near their peak nesting activities. Yet two or three thousand feet higher, only a few songbirds will be singing, and those have yet to establish a territory. Ice and snow may linger in the shadows on the north-facing slopes and new snowfall may occur on any given day. It will be the middle of June before the songbirds' nesting season is at its peak. Only then will every patch of blackberry have its pair of nesting Chestnut-sided Warblers, and the songs of Veerys and Winter Wrens cascade through the silent firs. Dark-eyed Juncos will seem to be everywhere, chipping their annoyance at your presence or scurrying to and fro with insect larvae for ever-hungry young.

Spring is an exciting time to bird in the park. Singing birds are abundant and it is a good time to learn to distinguish each species by its song. Every bird encountered is in its breeding plumage and is truly outstanding. A good birder who can identify most of the species by sight or sound, and who birds as many habitats as possible, can expect to find 100 species a day in late April and early May. Adding some of the agricultural and residential areas just outside the park will likely produce a few more species for the list.

Summer in the park is often a season of warm days and cool nights. When the temperatures reach the 80s or low 90s in Cades Cove, Gatlinburg, or Cherokee, you can drive up toward the Canadian zone and cooler temperatures. At Newfound Gap or one of the higher ridges, the temperature may be 15-20 degrees Fahrenheit cooler than in the valleys. Summer is the season of greatest visitor attendance in the park and it is also the period of greatest precipitation. Everything looks green and the mountain peaks are often veiled in the misty clouds that long ago gave the Great Smoky Mountains their name. Most birds in the lower elevations are busy with their fledglings or starting a second cycle of nesting activity, while those in the high elevations are engaged in bringing up their first brood of the year. Tree foliage is at its peak and so are the armies of insects that feed on leaves and are, in turn, part of the food chain of many birds.

In summer the evergreen heath plants burst into showy blossom. The mountain laurel and flame azalea begin their bloom in late April in the low elevations and continue on into May and June as the season climbs the slopes. The white to shell-pink flowers of the rosebay rhododendron begin to bloom in May and June on woody plants that may exceed 20 feet in height. The heath balds on the ridges from 3,000 feet to the highest crown are vast floral displays of purple rhododendron in June and July. Standing on a heath bald covered with bush after bush of purple rhododendron is quite an experience. Misty blue mountains march into the horizon and Chimney Swifts twitter overhead on rapidly beating wings. A Common Raven's hoarse *cronk* call floats across the space and you may see the large, jet-black bird soaring on set wings.

Eastern Towhees, Dark-eyed Juncos, Gray Catbirds, and Chestnut-sided Warblers sing from the shrubs and a Ruby-throated Hummingbird hovers on invisible wings before each open flower.

Fall is a time of restless change in the park. Many species of birds have raised their broods and molted their feathers. Warblers now wear the confusing fall plumage which so frustrates birders. Even as they settle into a comfortable roost for the night, many species of birds are restless, they stir and awaken, and on one particular night they leave their perch to migrate south. In mid-September the Broad-winged Hawks begin to kettle-up over the ridges and glide to the bottom of the next thermal, then rise again. Scores may go by in a day with Sharp-shinned Hawks, Coopers Hawks, Northern Harriers, and others. A good place to observe these migrating raptors is from the concrete fire tower at Look Rock on the Foothills Parkway just outside the northwest boundary of the park. Many of the park's summer residents depart for their wintering grounds further south in late August, September, and October. The warblers, vireos, orioles, Wood Thrush, Veery, tanagers, most flycatchers, and others steal away in the night. Yet even as they leave, winter visitors from the north begin to arrive. Soon one can count Hermit Thrush, Yellow-rumped Warbler, Swamp Sparrow, White-throated Sparrow, Purple Finch, Evening Grosbeak, and others in a day's birding.

Autumn's pageantry is a spectacular paintpot of color in these ancient mountains with their great variety of trees. The fall color season is a somewhat long affair that begins near the mountains' crests with yellow birch, mountain maple, and other deciduous trees and slowly descends into the valleys. The peak of the color season is often in the last two weeks of October when the days are clear and cool and the skies are a rich northern blue. It is a time when a cock Ruffed Grouse may stand on a favorite drumming log, raise his crest and ruff, fan his tail, and vigorously beat his wings against the air. As you climb these mountain trails, the drumming of the grouse sounds like it is coming from your own chest. It begins slowly and accelerates before fading into the distance; but at first notice it sounds as if your own heart is running away.

BIRDING IN THE PARK

The purpose of this book is to help further your enjoyment of birds by illustrating many of the more conspicuous species and to provide general information on when and where you are most likely to observe them. This book is not intended to be used as a field guide because most birders already own one. If not, field guides to birds are available at visitor centers in the park at Sugarlands, Oconaluftee, and Cades Cove. This book, therefore, lacks complete descriptions of all field marks, plumages, sexual differences, age differences, etc., common to such texts. However, there is enough information to allow you to identify and learn some of the local life history of the 100 species illustrated and to satisfy your natural curiosity of "what bird is that."

If you are birding the park from late spring through autumn, when dense foliage covers most of the forest, you will hear many more birds than you will see. The eastern deciduous forest is a difficult place for beginning birders who must rely on seeing birds to identify them. But, even if you don't recognize each bird by its voice, you can use the vocalizations to locate the bird and, with a little searching, obtain satisfying views of it.

Learning bird songs is a matter of repetition and experience; the more time you spend in the field the better you will become at identifying birds with your ears. Watching the bird as it sings is great reinforcement, especially when combined with reading the description of the bird's song in a field guide or listening to a recording of it.

Great Smoky Mountains National Park is a friendly place to walk in the out-of-doors and to birdwatch while enjoying all the beauty of this great natural area. There are a few dangers you should be mindful of, however.

WEATHER—The weather can change suddenly and frequently in the Smokies. The high elevations may receive 90 inches of precipitation annually and much of it comes during summer when the greatest numbers of visitors are in the park. Raingear is a must and should always be handy. Storms can be sudden and violent and lightning is often a major component. Open areas, especially in the high elevations and on exposed ridges, should be avoided at such times.

The winters can be cold, with subzero weather lingering in the high country for several days. Snowfall at the mountain crests is often measured annually in feet rather than inches. Warm clothing and proper boots are essential for comfort and protection during such periods. Talk to a park ranger about trail and hiking conditions before you set out to bird the high country in winter.

TRAILS—Stay on or very close to the trails. Don't leave them to bushwhack cross-country. The terrain is often steep, the vegetation is usually dense, and it is very easy to become lost in these mountains once you are off the trails. Don't wander. One person, or even a small party, can be extremely difficult to locate by trained rescuers in the vastness of this wilderness.

POISONOUS PLANTS—While there are several species of plants in the Smokies that are poisonous if eaten, only poison ivy (*Rhus radicans*) is poisonous to the touch. It is a fairly common plant below 3,000 feet and is often abundant along roadways, streambanks, fencerows, and in pine stands. It may be found as a ground cover or as a tree-climbing plant with hairy stems. The leaflets are almost always in threes, and the summer foliage is often a glossy green. All parts of the plant are poisonous and should be avoided. Several species of birds, including the Yellow-rumped Warbler, Eastern Bluebird, and Pileated Woodpecker, feed on the grayish-white berries.

POISONOUS REPTILES—Only two species of venomous reptiles occur in the park, the copperhead (*Agkistrodon contortrix*) and the timber rattlesnake (*Crotalus horridus*). The copperhead is considered to be uncommon in the Smokies, but there are places where it is plentiful (i.e., Rich Mountain bordering Cades Cove).

It is scarce or absent above 2,500 feet. Suitable habitats include rocky hillsides, stone fences, and the areas in and around abandoned buildings. In hot weather, both the copperhead and timber rattlesnake are mostly nocturnal. The timber rattlesnake is considered common and widespread and is found in all elevations from the lowest to Clingmans Dome, though it seldom enters the spruce-fir forests. Two color phases, yellow and black, occur in the park. Rocky hillsides, thick grassy areas, and rocky streamsides are all places that this rattlesnake frequents. Few visitors have encountered them on the trails and most snakes retreat when approached. Still, some individuals coil and stand their ground with rapidly buzzing tail when encountered. But don't depend on the rattlesnake to sound a warning; many don't rattle until they are physically disturbed. It will pay to watch where you are placing your feet if you wander around in the tall grasses on such high altitude meadows as Gregory Bald and Andrews Bald. Out of the millions of visitors to the park, almost none of them ever encounter a poisonous snake, and biologists and other researchers who spend hundreds of hours in the backcountry rarely locate one.

INSECTS—There are few biting insects in the park, but the warmer months bring a few mosquitoes and small gnats or "no-see-ums." Both are more common in the low elevations, but moderate applications of insect repellent should deter them. Periods from late morning to early evening in the summer are often free of these two insects.

BEARS—For most park visitors, even a brief glimpse of a black bear (*Ursus americanus*) is a highlight of their visit. These large omnivores are found at all elevations of the park and generally range in size from 125-300 pounds, though some individuals may weigh over 500 pounds. Bears may be encountered in any month from late March through mid-December. Even in winter a bear may rouse and take a short walk about in the snow before returning to the den. Bears are unpredictable and should always be observed from a safe distance. Most are truly wild and will scurry off as soon as they detect your presence. However those concentrated in the campground areas and sometimes along the roadways have come to associate people with handouts of food (strictly forbidden by park regulations) and are bolder. Adult females with cubs should be avoided as they can be protective of their young. Keep food up and out of reach if you camp in the backcountry, or locked inside your vehicle at night in the campgrounds. Enjoy the bears at a distance. Don't push your luck by getting closer.

HOW TO USE THIS BOOK . . . .

Take this book with you as you travel the park. It will help you locate and identify many of the birds that occur here during the year. The 100 birds chosen for illustration are all birds that are seasonally common or in some other way conspicuous, and, therefore, likely to be encountered by birders. Each bird pictured has a seasonal abundance status of either: abundant, common, fairly common, or uncommon (see the section titled "My Personal Checklist" for a description of the abundance codes). I have included those uncommon birds that have some feature that makes them conspicuous (large size, loud and far reaching voice, or habit of frequenting open areas). Birds such as the Wild Turkey, Great Horned Owl, and Red-tailed Hawk are in this category.

All species which have been reliably reported in the park are listed in "My Personal Checklist" in the order established by the American Ornithologists' Union (AOU). There is a space provided opposite each species on the list where you can check off the birds you find in the park. Additionally, the current seasonal abundance of each species is listed there. The arrangement of the illustrated species follows this general order also. The species descriptions feature the common name of the bird followed by its length in inches and centimeters (centimeters in parentheses) and the scientific name. All common and scientific names conform with the AOU Checklist of North American Birds, 7th Edition, 1998.

The length of the bird is measured from the tip of the bill to the tip of the longest tail feather. Lengths in this book are the average measurements compiled from standard sources from museum specimens. It is often enough to be able to compare the size of the unknown bird you are observing to that of a familiar species and continue your identification from there. Four general categories of size are all you will need in most situations: sparrow size (about six inches), robin size (approximately 10 inches), crow size (roughly 17 inches), and larger than a crow.

Seasonal distribution charts are provided for all 100 species illustrated. They provide a unique way of telling at a glance the approximate elevation in the park that the species should be expected to occur and at what season of the year it is expected there.

The numbers on the vertical axis (1-6) represent elevations from 1,000 to 6,000+ feet. The letters on the horizontal axis (S, W, M) represent the following: S = Summer (late April through early October); W = Winter (October through early April); M = Migration Seasons (April through May and September through early November).

The vertical bars on the charts tell you at what elevations and at what season each species of bird is most likely to occur. In cases where a bird is found year-round in the park at approximately the same elevations, a large block is used rather than individual bars. Two examples are given below.

The Black Vulture is most likely to occur at elevations below 3,000 feet throughout the year.

The Winter Wren is usually found at elevations above 4,500 feet in summer and below 3,000 feet in winter.

Birds of course are not bound by maps and one can always expect to find that individual bird who has not read this text and has turned up in an unexpected place. That's part of the excitement of birding. So, make a written record of your observation and turn it in to a park ranger. Change is to be expected in the park and as habitats are altered by natural succession, by changes in climate and airborne pollution, by insect infestations, fire and natural disturbances in the forests, the distribution of its birds may change also.

HOW TO FIND BIRDS . . . .

Birdwatching is a fascinating hobby that is enjoyed by millions of people in the United States. It provides all the lure and thrills of any outdoor sport and combines the challenge of locating birds with the identification of each species. As with any sport, you become more skilled with practice and experience. Quick and accurate identification of wild birds in their natural habitats requires learning fieldmarks, behaviors, songs and calls, plumage sequences, seasons of occurrence, and habitats. Today there are many excellent field guides to bird identification that make this activity much easier, and you can learn much about bird identification by just thumbing through such a book in the comfort of your home. Once you're in the field you will be engaged in a personally rewarding experience that you can continue at almost anytime, anywhere in the world.

The abundance of any species is tied to habitat. In summer, Chestnut-sided Warblers are common residents in the blackberry tangles and rhododendron thickets at the higher elevations. Looking for them anywhere else will almost never produce a Chestnut-sided Warbler. Similarly, the Eastern Meadowlark is a common resident in the open grassy meadows in Cades Cove and at Oconaluftee and is almost never found in any other habitat or location in the park. Learn to associate the bird with its preferred habitat and you will be much more successful.

In the Smokies, elevation influences abundance. The higher annual precipitation, cooler temperatures, and shorter growing seasons of the higher elevations determine the types of plant communities there. The spruce-fir forest supports breeding bird species that are common nowhere else in the park. Many species are altitudinally distributed.

Seasons of the year can also affect abundance. Scarlet Tanagers and Black-throated Green Warblers are common summer residents, but absent in the park from October to April. White-throated Sparrows winter here from late September into early May, then depart for more northern breeding areas. Many species are seen only in those few days or weeks when they are migrating through (see the checklist and the species accounts for more information on seasonal occurrence). Season can also affect the conspicuousness of birds. During the breeding season, many birds establish territories, attract mates, and threaten rival males with displays and vocalizations. These rites of spring make individual birds, particularly males, much easier to observe.

Time of day can also affect the numbers of birds you find. Early morning, especially the first hour of daylight, is the peak time of activity for most species. Mid-to-late afternoon usually produces another peak of activity, though not quite with the intensity of the morning. Midday, particularly in the heat of the summer, is often a time when the birds' activity slows and they are not as easily found. Some birds, like both species of vultures, often linger on the night's perch, stretching their wings and fanning their tails toward the sun, waiting for its heat to create the thermals that will help them slowly climb into the sky. Some are crepuscular, being most active at dawn and dusk. Others, like most owls and nightjars, are nocturnal and are most frequently heard calling after dark.

Bird as the experienced birders do. Walk quietly and learn to stand patiently as you look and listen for birds. Try to keep the sun at your back for the best lighting conditions. Many birders know that it is often possible to make inquisitive birds come into view, and to even approach you, if you make "pishing" or "squeaking" noises with your mouth or by loudly kissing the back of your hand. The calls of the Eastern Screech-Owl will frequently bring birds into view that are bent on finding this little predator. (You can learn to produce a whistled imitation of the owl's call or play a recording of it on a portable tape recorder.) Try not to make any sudden movements when the birds are coming in and you may get to see them up close for several minutes.

Remember you are in a national park, where all plants and animals are protected. Take care not to damage the habitat and take special care in the breeding season not to disturb the nesting activities of birds.

GUIDEBOOKS AND REFERENCES . . . .

The single best reference to the birds of the park is Arthur Stupka's *Notes on the Birds of Great Smoky Mountains National Park*, published by the University of Tennessee Press, Knoxville, 1963. Mr. Stupka was the park naturalist from 1935-60, and park biologist from 1960 until his retirement in 1963. This nonillustrated book was compiled from 28 years of his personal records and from many other reliable sources. It is the definitive natural history of every species of bird he considered to be reliably recorded in the park. As one would expect, the status of some species has changed, and some additional species have been recorded from the park in the more than 35 years since this work was published.

A checklist of the birds of Great Smoky Mountains National Park is available for a small fee at Great Smoky Mountains Association bookstores in all the park's visitor centers. You should find it useful for daily field trips during your stay here. (Any observations of rare or previously unreported species, or notes on breeding behavior or other facts of interest, should be reported on a Wildlife Observation Form, also available at visitor centers.)

There are several excellent field guides available that cover all the bird species found in the park. Some that I can recommend, in no particular order of preference, are:

National Geographic Society: Field Guide to the Birds of North America. 1983. National Geographic Society, Washington, D.C.

A Field Guide to the Birds of Eastern and Central North America. Roger Tory Peterson. 1980. Houghton Mifflin Company, Boston.

A *Guide to Field Identification: Birds of North America.*
Chandler S. Robbins, Bertel Bruun, and Herbert S. Zim. 1983.
Golden Press, New York.

EQUIPMENT . . . .

It is possible to birdwatch without a field guide, but not without binoculars. Most experienced birders use binoculars that are 7 ×, 8 ×, or 9 ×. This number refers to the magnification powers of the instrument and a 7 × binocular is one that optically brings an object seven times closer to you. Binoculars are categorized by the magnification coupled with a second number (i.e., 7 × 35), in which the "35" is the width of the front lens in millimeters. Even an inexpensive pair of binoculars will serve in letting you see birds well enough to identify and enjoy them. It takes a little practice in learning how to hold your eyes on the bird while bringing the binoculars up to them. Until you get the hang of it, practice on moving objects, large and small, and in short order you will be able to get even a bird in flight squarely in the field of view.

Telescopes are a useful additional piece of equipment. They allow you to see birds at a greater distance because of their higher magnifications (usually 15-60 power). Couple them with a tripod that is tall enough to let you stand and comfortably use the telescope and you will be able to see Wild Turkey a quarter mile away in Cades Cove or a hawk perched in a distant tree. Some telescopes can be combined with a camera as a telephoto lens.

A camera with a telephoto lens can be a great addition to your birding equipment. Many birds are quite colorful and make excellent photo subjects. However, most are relatively small and often will not allow a close approach. For bird photography a long lens, at least 300-400 mm, is an essential piece of equipment. A tripod or gunstock mount will help eliminate movement and sharpen the image. High shutter speeds are required for active birds. Films with an ASA of 200 or more are recommended for wildlife photography in the dark forests of the Smokies.

MY PERSONAL CHECKLIST
Birds of Great Smoky Mountains National Park

The common names used in this list conform with the American Ornithologist's Union Checklist of North American Birds, 7th Edition (1998).

STATUS CODE

A = Abundant: over 25 seen on a given day in proper habitat/season.

C = Common: 5-25 seen per day in proper habitat/season.

F = Fairly common: at least one individual per day in proper habitat/season.

U = Uncommon: at least one seen per season of occurrence or several seen per year.

O = Occasional: one seen per year or less.

X = Rare: has occurred in park at least once, but is not to be expected.

R = Permanent Resident
S = Summer Resident
W = Winter Resident
M = Migrant

SPECIAL NOTATIONS

* considered to breed within park
*? suspected to breed within park
cc = Cades Cove
lr = Look Rock fire tower
he = high elevation (above 3,500')
ri = reintroduced

LOONS
❏ Common Loon OM

GREBES
❏ Pied-billed Grebe UM
❏ Horned Grebe OM

STORM-PETRELS
❏ Band-rumped Storm Petrel XM

PELICANS & CORMORANTS
❏ American White Pelican XM
❏ Double-crested Cormorant XM

HERONS & VULTURES
- ❏ American Bittern OM
- ❏ Least Bittern OM
- ❏ Great Blue Heron UR cc
- ❏ Great Egret OM
- ❏ Little Blue Heron OM
- ❏ Green Heron FS* cc
- ❏ Black-crowned Night-Heron XS
- ❏ Yellow-crowned Night-Heron US* cc
- ❏ Black Vulture FR* cc
- ❏ Turkey Vulture CR* cc

GEESE & DUCKS
- ❏ Snow Goose XM
- ❏ Canada Goose UR*
- ❏ Brant XM
- ❏ Wood Duck OR* cc
- ❏ American Wigeon XM
- ❏ American Black Duck UW cc
- ❏ Mallard UW cc
- ❏ Blue-winged Teal UM, OW
- ❏ Northern Shoveler XM
- ❏ Northern Pintail XM
- ❏ Green-winged Teal XM
- ❏ Ring-necked Duck OW
- ❏ Lesser Scaup XM
- ❏ White-winged Scoter XW cc
- ❏ Black Scoter XW
- ❏ Bufflehead XW
- ❏ Common Goldeneye XW
- ❏ Hooded Merganser UW, XS cc
- ❏ Common Merganser OW
- ❏ Red-breasted Merganser XM
- ❏ Ruddy Duck OM cc

HAWKS & EAGLES
- ❏ Osprey OM
- ❏ Swallow-tailed Kite XS
- ❏ Mississippi Kite XM
- ❏ Bald Eagle OM
- ❏ Northern Harrier OMW
- ❏ Sharp-shinned Hawk UR*
- ❏ Cooper's Hawk UR*
- ❏ Northern Goshawk XR
- ❏ Red-shouldered Hawk OMW, OR*
- ❏ Broad-winged Hawk FS*, CM, lr
- ❏ Red-tailed Hawk UR*
- ❏ Golden Eagle XMW cc XS
- ❏ American Kestrel UR* cc
- ❏ Merlin XMS
- ❏ Peregrine Falcon OWM, OS* ri

GROUSE, TURKEYS & QUAILS
- ❏ Ruffed Grouse FR*
- ❏ Wild Turkey UR* cc
- ❏ Northern Bobwhite FR*

RAILS, GALLINULES, COOTS
- ❏ King Rail XMS
- ❏ Virginia Rail XM
- ❏ Sora OM
- ❏ Common Moorhen XM
- ❏ American Coot XMWS

CRANES
- [ ] Sandhill Crane XM

SHOREBIRDS
- [ ] American Golden-Plover XM
- [ ] Semipalmated Plover OM cc
- [ ] Killdeer UR* cc
- [ ] Greater Yellowlegs OM
- [ ] Lesser Yellowlegs XM
- [ ] Solitary Sandpiper UM
- [ ] Willet XM
- [ ] Spotted Sandpiper UM
- [ ] Semipalmated Sandpiper XM
- [ ] Least Sandpiper OM cc
- [ ] Ruff XM
- [ ] Common Snipe UMW cc
- [ ] American Woodcock UR*
- [ ] Red-necked Phalarope XM
- [ ] Red Phalarope XW

GULLS & TERNS
- [ ] Laughing Gull XM
- [ ] Bonaparte's Gull XM
- [ ] Ring-billed Gull XMW
- [ ] Herring Gull XW
- [ ] Sooty Tern XS

DOVES
- [ ] Rock Dove XR
- [ ] Mourning Dove CR* cc

CUCKOOS
- [ ] Black-billed Cuckoo US*
- [ ] Yellow-billed Cuckoo FS*

OWLS
- [ ] Barn Owl OR
- [ ] Eastern Screech-Owl FR*
- [ ] Great Horned Owl UR*
- [ ] Barred Owl FR*
- [ ] Northern Saw-whet Owl FR* he

NIGHTHAWKS & NIGHTJARS
- [ ] Common Nighthawk FM
- [ ] Chuck-will's-widow US
- [ ] Whip-poor-will FS*

SWIFTS & HUMMINGBIRDS
- [ ] Chimney Swift CS*
- [ ] Ruby-throated Hummingbird FS,* CM-fall

KINGFISHERS
- [ ] Belted Kingfisher FR*

WOODPECKERS
- [ ] Red-headed Woodpecker UR* cc
- [ ] Red-bellied Woodpecker FR*
- [ ] Yellow-bellied Sapsucker US,* he, FW
- [ ] Downy Woodpecker FR*
- [ ] Hairy Woodpecker FR*
- [ ] Red-cockaded Woodpecker OR* (formerly)
- [ ] Northern Flicker FR*
- [ ] Pileated Woodpecker FR*

FLYCATCHERS
- ❒ Olive-sided Flycatcher US,* he
- ❒ Eastern Wood-Pewee CS*
- ❒ Yellow-bellied Flycatcher XM
- ❒ Acadian Flycatcher CS*
- ❒ Alder Flycatcher OM
- ❒ Willow Flycatcher OS
- ❒ Least Flycatcher US*
- ❒ Eastern Phoebe CR* (UW)
- ❒ Great Crested Flycatcher FS*
- ❒ Western Kingbird XM
- ❒ Eastern Kingbird FS* cc
- ❒ Scissor-tailed Flycatcher XM cc

SHRIKES
- ❒ Loggerhead Shrike OR cc

VIREOS
- ❒ White-eyed Vireo FS*
- ❒ Yellow-throated Vireo CS*
- ❒ Blue-headed Vireo CS* he
- ❒ Warbling Vireo OS
- ❒ Philadelphia Vireo OM
- ❒ Red-eyed Vireo AS*

JAYS, CROWS, & RAVENS
- ❒ Blue Jay CR*
- ❒ American Crow CR*
- ❒ Common Raven FR* he

LARKS
- ❒ Horned Lark OR cc

SWALLOWS
- ❒ Purple Martin US
- ❒ Tree Swallow OM
- ❒ Northern Rough-winged Swallow FS*
- ❒ Bank Swallow OM
- ❒ Cliff Swallow UM
- ❒ Barn Swallow CS*

CHICKADEES & TITMICE
- ❒ Carolina Chickadee CR*
- ❒ Black-capped Chickadee FR* he
- ❒ Tufted Titmouse CR*

NUTHATCHES & CREEPERS
- ❒ Red-breasted Nuthatch CR* he
- ❒ White-breasted Nuthatch FR*
- ❒ Brown Creeper FR* he

WRENS
- ❒ Carolina Wren CR*
- ❒ Bewick's Wren XR* (formerly OR*)
- ❒ House Wren OR, FM
- ❒ Winter Wren CR* he
- ❒ Sedge Wren OM
- ❒ Marsh Wren OM

KINGLETS
- ❒ Golden-crowned Kinglet CR* he
- ❒ Ruby-crowned Kinglet FMW

GNATCATCHERS
- ❒ Blue-gray Gnatcatcher CS*

THRUSHES
- [ ] Eastern Bluebird FR* cc
- [ ] Veery CS* he
- [ ] Gray-cheeked Thrush FM
- [ ] Swainson's Thrush CM
- [ ] Hermit Thrush FW, US (*?)
- [ ] Wood Thrush CS*
- [ ] American Robin FR,* CM

THRASHERS
- [ ] Gray Catbird FS,* OW
- [ ] Northern Mockingbird UR*
- [ ] Brown Thrasher FS,* UW

STARLINGS
- [ ] European Starling CR*

PIPITS & WAXWINGS
- [ ] American Pipit OWM
- [ ] Cedar Waxwing FR* (erratic)

WOOD-WARBLERS
- [ ] Blue-winged Warbler FM
- [ ] Golden-winged Warbler US*
- [ ] Brewster's Warbler XM
- [ ] Lawrence's Warbler XM
- [ ] Tennessee Warbler CM
- [ ] Orange-crowned Warbler OMW
- [ ] Nashville Warbler FM
- [ ] Northern Parula FS*
- [ ] Yellow Warbler FS*
- [ ] Chestnut-sided Warbler CS* he
- [ ] Magnolia Warbler CM (*?)
- [ ] Cape May Warbler FM
- [ ] Black-throated Blue Warbler CS,* he
- [ ] Yellow-rumped Warbler A-CMW
- [ ] Black-throated Green Warbler CS*
- [ ] Blackburnian Warbler FS* he
- [ ] Yellow-throated Warbler FS*
- [ ] Pine Warbler FS,* OW
- [ ] Prairie Warbler US*
- [ ] Palm Warbler FM, OW
- [ ] Bay-breasted Warbler FM
- [ ] Blackpoll Warbler FM (spr.), OM (fall)
- [ ] Cerulean Warbler FM, OS
- [ ] Black-and-white Warbler CS*
- [ ] American Redstart FS*
- [ ] Prothonotary Warbler OM, XS*
- [ ] Worm-eating Warbler FS*
- [ ] Swainson's Warbler US*
- [ ] Ovenbird CS*
- [ ] Northern Waterthrush OM
- [ ] Louisiana Waterthrush CS*
- [ ] Kentucky Warbler CS*
- [ ] Connecticut Warbler OM
- [ ] Common Yellowthroat FS*
- [ ] Hooded Warbler CS*
- [ ] Wilson's Warbler OM
- [ ] Canada Warbler CS* he
- [ ] Yellow-breasted Chat US*

TANAGERS
- [ ] Summer Tanager FS*
- [ ] Scarlet Tanager CS*

SPARROWS
- ❒ Eastern Towhee CR*
- ❒ Bachman's Sparrow XS (formerly OS)
- ❒ Chipping Sparrow CS*
- ❒ Field Sparrow CR*
- ❒ Vesper Sparrow UM cc
- ❒ Lark Sparrow XS cc
- ❒ Savannah Sparrow UMW cc
- ❒ Grasshopper Sparrow OSM cc
- ❒ Henslow's Sparrow XM
- ❒ Le Conte's Sparrow XMW cc
- ❒ Fox Sparrow O-FW
- ❒ Song Sparrow CR*
- ❒ Lincoln's Sparrow OM
- ❒ Swamp Sparrow FW
- ❒ White-throated Sparrow C-AW
- ❒ White-crowned Sparrow OM, OW
- ❒ Dark-eyed Junco AR* he (lower elev. W)
- ❒ Snow Bunting XW he

CARDINALS, GROSBEAKS & BUNTINGS
- ❒ Northern Cardinal CR*
- ❒ Rose-breasted Grosbeak FS* he
- ❒ Blue Grosbeak OM, OS cc (*?)
- ❒ Indigo Bunting C-AS*
- ❒ Dickcissel XW cc

MEADOWLARKS, BLACKBIRDS, & ORIOLES
- ❒ Bobolink UM cc
- ❒ Red-winged Blackbird FM, CS,* cc, UW
- ❒ Eastern Meadowlark CR* cc
- ❒ Rusty Blackbird UM, OW
- ❒ Common Grackle FS,* UW
- ❒ Brown-headed Cowbird FM, FR*
- ❒ Orchard Oriole UM, US*
- ❒ Baltimore Oriole UM, OS,* cc

FINCHES
- ❒ Purple Finch U-FW
- ❒ House Finch XW, OR
- ❒ Red Crossbill UR he (erratic) (*?)
- ❒ White-winged Crossbill XW
- ❒ Common Redpoll XW
- ❒ Pine Siskin US, U-CW (erratic) (*?)
- ❒ American Goldfinch FR*
- ❒ Evening Grosbeak U-CW (erratic)

OLD WORLD SPARROWS
- ❒ House Sparrow UR*

Reference: 7th edition (1998) of the AOU Checklist of North American Birds.

THE TOPOGRAPHY OF A BIRD

Primaries —————

Trailing edge —————

Secondaries —

Wing lining —————
Uppertail coverts —————
Rump —————
Undertail coverts —————

Flank —————

Side —————
Belly —————

Breast —————

Tarsus —————

RAY HARM

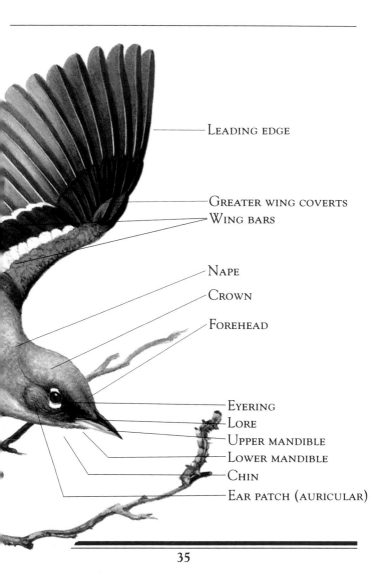

LEADING EDGE

GREATER WING COVERTS
WING BARS

NAPE

CROWN

FOREHEAD

EYERING
LORE
UPPER MANDIBLE
LOWER MANDIBLE
CHIN
EAR PATCH (AURICULAR)

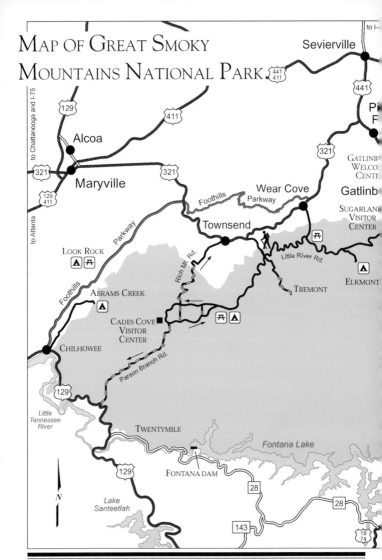

MAP OF GREAT SMOKY MOUNTAINS NATIONAL PARK

to I-

Sevierville

441
411

to Chattanooga and I-75

129

411

441

Alcoa

Pi
F

321

321

321

GATLINB
WELCO
CENTE

Maryville

Foothills Parkway

Wear Cove

Gatlinb

129
411

to Atlanta

Parkway

Townsend

SUGARLAN
VISITOR
CENTER

Little River Rd.

LOOK ROCK

Rich Mt. Rd.

ELKMONT

ABRAMS CREEK

TREMONT

Foothills

CADES COVE
VISITOR
CENTER

CHILHOWEE

Parson Branch Rd.

129

Little
Tennessee
River

TWENTYMILE

Fontana Lake

N

129

FONTANA DAM

28

Lake
Santeetlah

28

143

19
74

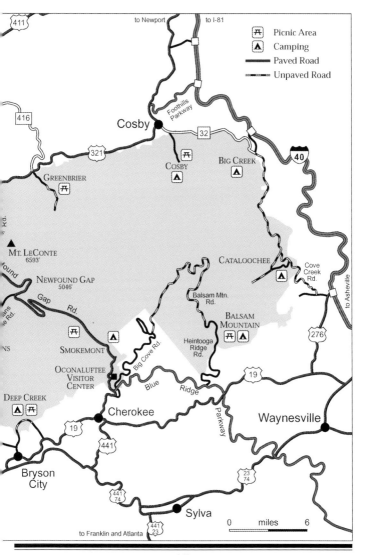

411

to Newport   to I-81

🏕 Picnic Area
🔺 Camping
━━━ Paved Road
▪▪▪ Unpaved Road

416

Cosby

Foothills Parkway

32

321

🏕 COSBY

BIG CREEK

I-40

🔺

GREENBRIER

🏕

▲ MT. LECONTE
6593'

CATALOOCHEE

Cove Creek Rd.

NEWFOUND GAP
5046'

🔺

Gap   Rd.

Balsam Mtn. Rd.

BALSAM MOUNTAIN

🏕 🔺

276

to Asheville

🏕   🔺

SMOKEMONT

Heintooga Ridge Rd.

19

OCONALUFTEE VISITOR CENTER

Big Cove Rd.

DEEP CREEK
🔺 🏕

Blue   Ridge

Cherokee

Parkway

Waynesville

19

441

23
74

Bryson City

Sylva

441
74

441
23

to Franklin and Atlanta

0   miles   6

GREEN HERON

Butorides striatus
18 in (46 cm)

Fred J. Alsop III

This small, chunky heron is the most common heron in the park. It is usually seen as a solitary individual or in pairs from early April into late October. The bird is about the size of a crow and in flight it is often mistaken for one. On closer inspection, a flying heron looks like a crow with a lump in its throat.

Search for the Green Heron along the banks of the larger streams below 2,500 feet in the park. Check in summer along the Oconaluftee River near the visitor center, near park headquarters at Sugarlands, and in Cades Cove. Cades Cove is perhaps the best place in the Smokies to see the bird, especially along Abrams Creek. Some of the best places in Cades Cove are the oxbow area of Abrams Creek about one-half mile upstream from the turnoff to the Abrams Falls parking area, and the "gum swamp" just east of the Cable Mill.

When searching for food (insects, small reptiles, frogs, salamanders, and small fish), the heron moves very slowly. It creeps along the stream bank or pond edge and stands with neck drawn back for minutes on end ready to strike with lightning speed. The bird often perches on tree branches and usually flies up to another tree when startled.

Coragyps atratus
25 in (64 cm)

G. Ron Austing

BLACK VULTURE

This fairly common resident should be looked for among the Turkey Vultures, especially in the lower elevations of the park. The Black Vulture is smaller and flaps its wings more in flight than the Turkey Vulture, often alternating between soaring and three or four rapid wing beats. Its silhouette in flight is similar to a hawk's. At close range look for the large white wing tips.

Vultures have necks and heads bare of feathers, a fact that has evolved as a result of their feeding habits. Their feet are too weak to tear apart their prey in the manner of hawks and owls, so this is done with the mandibles, often with the bird's head inside the body cavity of the dead animal. Bacteria, protozoans, and other potential threats to the vulture's health are quickly killed by exposure to sunlight. Though the Black Vulture is a carrion feeder like the Turkey Vulture, it has been known to kill small animals in the manner of a hawk.

The Black Vulture is not as light on the wing as the larger Turkey Vulture and it often leaves the park in the late fall for the warmer air and lifting thermals of more southern states. This species lacks the keen sense of smell of the Turkey Vulture and seems less efficient at locating carrion. It often follows its cousins as they flock to a meal and then aggressively nudges them away from it.

TURKEY VULTURE

Cathartes aura
27 in (69 cm)

Fred J. Alsop III

One of the largest birds in the park, the Turkey Vulture soars on wings that span six feet. The Turkey Vulture is a fairly common to common permanent resident that may be seen at any elevation, but is most often found over open areas in the lowlands. Cades Cove is the best place to observe this bird. You can identify this bird by the V-angle of the wings over the back as it glides in lazy circles. Closer observation will reveal two additional identifying marks; the two-toned effect of the wing, dark in front and silver-gray behind, and the long rectangular tail extending beyond the trailing feet.

For many years there has been a favorite roosting tree in Cades Cove located on Hyatt Lane, the unpaved road at marker #6, just beyond the Methodist Church. The tree is a large white pine with the top blown out. It stands in the woodlot to the left (approximately ¼ mile from the road) just before you cross the first small stream. Turkey Vultures, and sometimes Black Vultures, are seen perched on or flying in the general vicinity of this tree.

Vultures are usually not up and soaring at daylight. Rather, they remain perched for several hours preening their feathers and "sunbathing" with their wings spread-eagle. This is the most commonly seen large soaring bird at all elevations of the park at any time of year.

Accipiter striatus
Male—10 in (25 cm)
Female—14 in (36 cm)

SHARP-SHINNED HAWK

Fred J. Alsop III

The Sharp-shinned Hawk is the smallest of the park's Accipiters or bird-eating hawks. Though it is a resident, it is seldom observed because of its preference for haunting woodland areas and spending most of its time beneath the tree canopy. More than half of the records of this hawk in the park have been made during fall migration (from mid-September into November) when birds from the northern states and Canada pass through the Smokies.

Birds of prey often show noticeable differences in size between the two sexes, with the females being up to one-third larger than the males. Ornithologists believe this size difference allows the two sexes to feed on prey of different sizes and, therefore, not compete with each other for food.

Sharp-shinned Hawks are very similar in appearance to the larger Cooper's Hawk (*A. cooperii*) and there is an overlap in size between female Sharp-shins and male Cooper's hawks. Both species have short, rounded wings and a long tail, but the tail appears squared or notched on the end in Sharp-shins and rounded in the Cooper's. The flight of both species is distinctive, with the birds alternating between a few quick, powerful wing beats and a short glide. The Sharp-shinned Hawk shows a preference for stands of conifers at all elevations in the park.

BROAD-WINGED HAWK

Buteo platypterus
Male—15 in (38 cm)
Female—17 in (43 cm)

G. Ron Austing

The Broad-winged Hawk is a fairly common summer resident seen at all elevations. This migratory bird usually arrives in the first two weeks of April and the breeding population is probably gone by early September. In the last two weeks of September, southward migrating flocks of this hawk can sometimes be seen. The best areas in the park to watch for fall flights are vantage points in the higher elevations, including Newfound Gap, Indian Gap, and Clingmans Dome. Another good place to watch these hawks and other species in migration is from the Look Rock fire tower on the Foothills Parkway.

This is a bird of the deciduous woodlands which often hunts from low perches. I have frequently seen these hawks hunting along the trans-mountain road between Gatlinburg and Cherokee. The broadly banded dark and white tail is characteristic, with the white bands being about equal in width to the dark ones.

During its summer stay with us, I have often been made aware of the Broad-wing's presence by its thin, shrill *pee-weeeee* whistled call.

Buteo jamaicensis
Male—20 in (52 cm)
Female—22 in (56 cm)

RED-TAILED HAWK

G. Ron Austing

There is a noted scarcity of hawks in the Southern Appalachians. The Red-tailed Hawk is perhaps the most commonly observed hawk in the park, but, when compared to many species of songbirds, it is not a common bird. This bird of prey occurs at all elevations in the Smokies and is most often seen soaring in spiraling circles at heights from just above the treetops to high above the ridges. When it perches on a fence post or the top of some favorite tree, it is easily overlooked. The open, gently rolling fields of Cades Cove are the best places to find the birds in any season. The short, fan-shaped tail with its bright rust-colored upperside and the dark, heavily streaked belly band are the clinching field marks. More a bird of the open woods and fields than of the closed forests, the Red-tail frequents the breaks in the canopy where it catches small mammals, the staple in its diet. It is a permanent resident that nests in the park.

If you follow the excited *cawing* of the American Crow, you will often find that a Red-tail has caused the commotion. Crows seem to take a special delight in mobbing hawks and owls, and the large Red-tailed Hawk is no exception.

AMERICAN KESTREL (Sparrow Hawk)

Falco sparverius
Male—9 in (24 cm)
Female—11 in (28 cm)

Fred J. Alsop III

This small falcon nests in tree cavities and man-made structures. It is a permanent resident that has been seen at all elevations, but is most common in open areas in the lower elevations. The best places to look are Cades Cove, Cataloochee, and Oconaluftee. More observations have been made of this species in the winter months, when local populations are swelled by individuals coming in from the north, than at any other season. As with other birds of prey, the female is larger than her mate and her plumage is noticeably different. Males have a reddish back and tail contrasting with bluish-gray wings, while the brownish back and barred tail of the female are the same color as her wings. The bird often hunts by hovering with its almost vertically positioned body suspended motionless between rapidly beating wings.

The name kestrel is derived from the Latin *crepicella*, "to rattle, creak, or crackle," which is suggestive of its call. The old common name, Sparrow Hawk, is more in reference to the bird's small size than to its prey, for it feeds more commonly on large insects and small rodents than on birds. The kestrel frequents open country and is more common in the cultivated and pastured valleys outside the park, where rural utility lines often serve as favorite lookout perches.

Falco peregrinus
Male—16 in (41 cm)
Female—20 in (51 cm)

PEREGRINE FALCON

Fred J. Alsop III

The Peregrine Falcon is truly one of the most spectacular birds of prey in the world. It feeds on other birds that it takes in midair with a powerful dive that may reach speeds in excess of 180 mph. Until the early 1940s, the Peregrine was a permanent resident and a breeding species in the park with nesting sites on Peregrine Peak. The use of pesticides, especially DDT, completely extirpated this falcon from its entire eastern U.S. breeding range by the 1970s. For several years in the 1980s, young Peregrines were released from a hacking tower in the northeastern part of the park in the hope that the species would once again be established here. In 1990, two adult birds returned to Peregrine Peak.

This is a large bird of prey with a wingspan of 36–44 inches. It has the long pointed wings and long tail typical of a falcon.

The nests of earlier years were shallow scrapes on cliff ledges. Often the feathers of prey species were found near these sites, called eyries, and in the Smokies included such birds as robins, other thrush species, juncos, Blue Jays, mergansers, and bitterns. Any observations of this species should be reported to a park ranger.

45

RUFFED GROUSE

Bonasa umbellus
17 in (43 cm)

G. Ron Austing

The Ruffed Grouse is a permanent resident that occurs at all elevations in the park. It is perhaps most commonly seen as it frequents the grassy margins along the roadsides. You'll have more luck finding birds along the road early in the morning before the traffic causes the grouse to seek the more sheltered woodlands it prefers. The most commonly heard sound is one produced by the male's "drumming" of the air with quick wingbeats as he stands on a favorite log or perch. At a distance, this low booming gives more the effect of a pulsation or throb in the air than a distinct sound. It starts slowly with widely spaced beats that increase in frequency until they become a muffled roar that fades out as it ends. It is a sound that seems to come from within the listener, as if one's own heart is racing out of rhythm as you walk upward in the thin mountain air. Drumming has been recorded in every month by these almost solitary birds, but strangely, the greatest number of reports have been in October, well after the breeding season.

Nesting takes place in the park in mid-April and May in the lower elevations, progressing into June in the higher ones. The nest is on the ground. There has been some concern in recent years about the possible effect the non-native wild hog has on the nesting success of the Ruffed Grouse and the Wild Turkey.

Meleagris gallopavo
Male—46 in (117 cm)
Female—37 in (94 cm)

WILD TURKEY

G. Ron Austing

This uncommon permanent resident is the largest bird in the park. It occurs at all elevations and tends to shy away from the places most frequented by man. It prefers open woodlands, the borders of fields, and forest clearings. Perhaps the best place to see this magnificent bird is in Cades Cove. Within the cove, look carefully along the edges where treeline and open field meet. The fields near the Methodist Church in the cove have been the "hot" spots for Turkey in recent years.

Most of the gobbling and strutting by the males occurs from late March through May, and can be heard from almost a mile away. The spring courtship often involves several females in close company with a strutting cock. He droops his wings until their tips almost drag the ground and spreads his chestnut-tipped tail wide.

Search in Cades Cove for our largest American gamebird and Benjamin Franklin's choice for America's national emblem. Your best opportunities are on those days when few visitors are out in the fields or early in the morning before many people are in the cove. While individual birds or small flocks can sometimes be seen in the open fields, I have more often found them by scanning the forest floor along the edges of the woodlots.

NORTHERN BOBWHITE

Colinus virginianus
9¾ in (25 cm)

S. J. Lang/Vireo

This permanent resident seems to be decreasing in numbers as forested areas overtake the clearings of pre-park days. In places like Cades Cove, where open meadowlands are maintained, the *bobwhite* call is still commonly heard. I have observed these birds in the higher elevations of the park on some of the balds, especially Andrews Bald and Spence Field. Birds are most often seen as single individuals in the late spring and summer months. You may almost step on the birds concealed in the grass before they suddenly flutter away on whirring wings.

Open brushy fields provide excellent foraging, nesting, and roosting habitat for bobwhite. Running and walking are a way of life for the "quail," for they seem to prefer this mode of locomotion to flying. The birds have a most interesting roosting pattern when they are in their coveys in the nonbreeding seasons. They enter their night's roost with the covey in a tight circle, all the birds backed in like the numerous spokes of a wheel, ready for instant flight in all directions should danger approach.

Scolopax minor
11 in (28 cm)

AMERICAN WOODCOCK

G. Ron Austing

This secretive nocturnal bird is an uncommon permanent resident in the park, but it is probably more common than the infrequent observations would indicate. The American Woodcock is a chunky, long-billed bird whose mottled brown plumage blends in perfectly with the leaves of the forest floor.

Woodcocks have been observed at all elevations in the park, but they prefer moist woodlands, thickets, and tall grass fields where their main food, earthworms, are most common. Most of the park records are from the lower elevations, but there are enough high elevation sightings from roadsides and the grassy balds during June and July to indicate the bird may also be breeding in these high mountain habitats.

The woodcock may begin its courtship as early as January and continue its vocalizations and displays into early May in the lower elevations. The male begins an elaborate flight display in which he circles high in the night sky before spiraling back to earth. During the descent he constantly twitters while specialized feathers on his wings produce a whistling sound. I have slipped quietly closer and closer to such courting males in the semidarkness until I sat within a few feet of a displaying bird so intent on his courtship calling that I went unnoticed.

MOURNING DOVE

Zenaida macroura
12 in (31 cm)

Fred J. Alsop III

Most of the sightings of this species come from below 2,000 feet, primarily along the roadsides and such open areas as Sugarlands, Cades Cove, Oconaluftee, and Cataloochee. One of the earliest nesters of all the park's birds, this dove has been seen in its billing and cooing courtship antics as early as February. This strong, rapid flier lays two whitish eggs at each nesting. Its nest is a stick structure so poorly constructed that the eggs can often be seen right through the bottom.

Mourning Doves, like other doves and pigeons, regurgitate food to their nestlings. For the first few days of their lives this food is "pigeon's milk," a creamy substance that is produced from epithelial cells shed from the lining of the crop. From about the fifth day on, seeds and insects are gradually added to the milk. These doves may nest as many as five times in a single breeding season, which can last into September.

The common name is in reference to the low, mournful *coos* produced by the bird, a call that is so low-pitched that it is sometimes mistaken for the hooting of an owl. The Mourning Dove is a permanent resident of the park.

YELLOW-BILLED CUCKOO

Coccyzus americanus
12 in (31 cm)

G. Ron Austing

Although this is a fairly common summer resident in woodlands below 3,500 feet, you will hear many more than you see. The bird is large, but easily missed as it moves with slothful purpose from branch to branch in the interior of a tree or bush. The cuckoo arrives in late April and is usually gone by the middle of October. Most of the guttural song is heard from mid-June well into August. The locals know it as the "rain crow" because the singing is thought to signal coming showers.

At close range the yellow lower bill will identify this cuckoo, but at greater distances look for the double row of large white spots beneath the tail and the rufous flash of the wing against the browner body in flight. It is not a brood parasite like the many species of cuckoos in the Old World. Cuckoos are one of the few species in the park that will eat tent caterpillars. Trees with these distinctive white tents should be given a second look for the presence of this bird.

EASTERN SCREECH-OWL

Otus asio
8½ in (22 cm)

Fred J. Alsop III

This is a fairly common permanent resident in woodlands below 4,000 feet. Eastern Screech-Owls may be reddish, brown, or gray in their plumage and in the park the reddish phase outnumbers the gray by approximately four to one; brown-plumaged birds are extremely rare. Like most owls, this one is active at night and often frequents roadsides; a habit that has made it the most frequently road-killed bird in the Smokies. The song is not a screech as the name implies, but a quavering whistle that often descends in pitch near the end. It has been heard at all months of the year, but most often in March and from July through October. If you can imitate this bird's call, you will have a good chance of getting Eastern Screech-Owls to answer and sometimes come silently into view. In daylight hours the call will also attract many species of scolding songbirds in search of the "owl."

Screech-owls often roost in tree cavities during the day or seek cover deep in the foliage where they remain as inconspicuous as possible. Any one who has walked the woods here has probably passed close by an owl without ever suspecting they were being constantly viewed through the narrowly slitted lids of a screech-owl's eyes.

Strix varia
Male—17 in (43 cm)
Female—21 in (53 cm)

BARRED OWL

Fred J. Alsop III

This is the hoot owl of Southern swamplands, a fairly common permanent resident recorded at all elevations. It is the most frequently heard owl in the high elevation forests, especially in the summer months. Its range is such that it is most common in the high elevations, least common in the middle elevations, and common once again in the lower regions such as Cades Cove. The call of the Barred Owl has often been described as *Who cooks for you? Who cooks for youall?* The lack of "horns," brown eyes, and the barring on the upper breast serve to distinguish this species.

Barred Owls are often active in the daytime and their distinctive calls can sometimes be heard then. It seems to be a most inquisitive owl, or at least one that is curious about any other "barred owl" in its territory. It will often respond to even a poor imitation of its call by answering back and even coming closer for a look. I have gotten these owls to answer my imitation during both day and night in the spruce-fir forests near Newfound Gap, Indian Gap, and Clingmans Dome. I've also had luck in the southern hardwoods of Cherokee Orchard, Sugarlands, and Cades Cove. This is probably the most frequently encountered owl in the Smokies.

NORTHERN SAW-WHET OWL

Aegolius acadicus
7 in (18 cm)

Fred J. Alsop III

The first report of this small northern owl's occurrence in the park was made in 1941. Its presence has lured and excited many birders since, but none has found hard evidence that this bird nests here (although juvenile birds have been sighted on Gregory Bald in the summer). Still, it is present and seems to be territorial during the breeding season. Most of the observations have been made in the high elevations, principally in the Canadian zone spruce-fir forests.

The Northern Saw-whet is named for the quality of its monotonous whistled song which, to the ornithologist who named it, sounded like someone sharpening (whetting) a saw. The best times to hear the song are from the first week of April through May. The birds sing from just after dark throughout the night. Moonlit nights seem more productive than dark ones, and if there is wind, rain, or fog—forget it—as the birds seldom sing under such conditions. The best places are the pull-offs between Newfound Gap and Clingmans Dome parking areas with "hot" spots in recent years being Indian Gap and the parking area of the Spruce-Fir Nature Trail. It is not difficult to hear a bird in the right season, but they are hard to see, even though they allow close approaches. This is the smallest owl in the park and it lacks the "horned" ear tufts of the slightly larger screech-owl.

Caprimulgus vociferus
9¾ in (25 cm)

WHIP-POOR-WILL

G. Ron Austing

A fairly common summer resident below 3,000 feet, this bird can
be heard calling from such campgrounds as Cosby, Smokemont, Elkmont,
and Cades Cove. It sings from dusk well into the night and again at
dawn. Another good spot is the road between Metcalf Bottoms Picnic
Area and the park boundary near Wear Cove. The birds begin singing
when they arrive around the first of April and continue into late July.
They are difficult to observe and are known chiefly by their call, a loud
whip-poor-will. The genus, *Caprimulgus*, is derived from the Latin *capri*,
"goat," and *mulgere*, "to milk." For some reason these birds have, for
many centuries (since at least Aristotle's time), been accused of clinging
to the udders of goats for food—a practice that was said to cause the
udder to wither and the goat to go blind. The bird's food consists entirely
of insects, most of which it catches in flight.

Natural reforestation has been occurring since the park was established
in the 1930s, particularly in the lowlands where this species is most
numerous. As the once-cleared areas begin to disappear, the Whip-poor-
will seems to be less common.

CHIMNEY SWIFT

Chaetura pelagica
5 in (12.5 cm)

G. Ron Austing

Chimney Swifts are common summer residents at all elevations and all habitats. This little, short-tailed bird, looking like a "cigar with wings" can be seen in flight during almost any daylight hour from the first week of April through the first week of October. The sooty-gray, stumpy-tailed birds dash above on rapidly flickering wings as they catch insects in midair. They have been found nesting in chimneys, once on the inside wall of a building, and inside the cavities of trees—their ancestral nesting place. Our attention is usually first drawn to them by their sharp twittering calls as they wheel overhead. The nest, which will hold three to six white eggs, is made of small twigs the swifts break off branches with their feet as they fly past.

Swift nestlings take a long time to mature adequately to leave their nest, an average of about 19 days. Nine to 12 days is enough for many similar-sized songbirds. However, even before their eyes have opened, swifts can cling to the nest with their feet, or even to the vertical structure the nest is attached to.

This is one of the most familiar birds to most people living in eastern North America and many can identify the "chimney sweep." Few have seen it closely, however, and it was not until the 1940s that scientists knew where it spent the winter: the Amazon Basin of South America.

RUBY-THROATED HUMMINGBIRD

Archilochus colubris
3¾ in (10 cm)

G. Bailey/Vireo

This is the smallest bird in the park and a fairly common summer resident which occurs at all elevations. Look for it from mid-April through mid-October. It is attracted to flowers, especially red, tubular-shaped ones, and it also seems to frequent streamside vegetation. When purple rhododendron (*Rhododendron catawbiense*) is in flower in the high elevations in mid-June, this bird can be found hovering before the blossoms. Only the adult male has the bright red throat. The nest is small (you could cover its top with a quarter) and contains two pea-sized white eggs.

The metabolized sugars from its diet are pumped through the small body by a heart that may beat more than 600 times a minute. The energy is burned so rapidly the bird must become torpid at night to conserve enough energy to survive until morning. The hum of the wings, stroking the air more than 70 times a second, and the squeaky chipping notes are often the first indication of the bird's presence.

If you visit the park in late summer or early fall when the cardinal flower (*Lobelia cardinalis*) is in bloom, take a few minutes and scan the stands of red blossoms beside low elevation streams. Your patience will almost surely be rewarded by the sight of a feeding Ruby-throated Hummingbird.

BELTED KINGFISHER

Ceryle alcyon
13 in (33 cm)

G. Ron Austing

There are more than 1,000 miles of streams in the park, and the Belted Kingfisher is a fairly common permanent resident along most of the larger ones below 3,000 feet. Look for it along Little River as you drive from Sugarlands Visitor Center to the Townsend "Y." There the bird can be seen hovering or flying a few feet above the surface, or perched motionless on some branch that provides a good view of the waters below.

The fish it feeds on are caught during a plunge that takes the kingfisher completely underwater. Abrams Creek is also an accessible spot to watch for this slate-backed bird. The female is the more colorful of the sexes with a chestnut breast band in addition to the gray one shared by the male. Nests are excavated by tunneling into dirt banks.

Kingfishers tend to be solitary birds except during the nesting season. Often one's attention is first attracted by their loud, rattling call. After catching a small fish, a kingfisher will fly with it to a nearby perch and bang it several times on the branch. If the fish is not to be transported back to waiting youngsters, the kingfisher will position the fish, often by a gentle toss in the air, so it can be swallowed headfirst.

RED-BELLIED WOODPECKER

Melanerpes carolinus
9¼ in (24 cm)

G. Ron Austing

This medium-sized, ladder-backed woodpecker is a fairly common permanent resident in the broad-leaved forests of the middle and lower elevations. Though it is a common species in the cutover woodlots surrounding the park, it is sometimes hard to locate within the boundaries, especially in the summer. Locations where the bird is seen with some regularity are the campgrounds in the lowlands, Metcalf Bottoms Picnic Area, and Sugarlands Visitor Center. The Red-bellied is a noisy bird and its varied calls are of a soft, scolding character. In flight look for the large white wing patches and the white rump as good field marks.

Many visitors mistakenly call this species a "red-headed woodpecker" because of the red forehead, crown, and nape of the male (females have red on the nape only). The Red-headed Woodpecker (*Melanerpes erythrocephalus*) is a very different looking bird with its entire head, neck, and throat a bright red. One has to inspect a Red-bellied Woodpecker at close range or through binoculars to see the small patch of dull red feathers on its belly and extending down between its legs.

YELLOW-BELLIED SAPSUCKER

Sphyrapicus varius
8½ in (22 cm)

J. R. Woodward/Vireo

Sapsuckers are permanent residents in the park. There is a breeding race that is present in the summer and is chiefly confined to the hardwood forests above 3,500 feet. These birds are uncommon and rather localized so that adding a sapsucker to your list between late April and the last of September is a difficult task. In late September, wintering birds from the North and many of the breeding birds begin to move into the low to middle elevations and sapsuckers are much more easily found. Evidence of the bird's presence, however, is abundant. There is scarcely a species of tree in the region that does not bear the distinctive rows of small, shallow drill holes made by these birds as they feed. The sapsucker feeds on the inner bark of trees, and returns later to eat the bleeding sap and the insects that have been attracted to it.

The long, white shoulder patch is characteristic. The yellowish underparts that give this sapsucker its name are brighter yellow in adult males than in females and juvenile birds. The sapsucker produces several squeaky call notes, but one of the most distinctive is a catlike *mew.*

Picoides pubescens
6¾ in (17 cm)

DOWNY WOODPECKER

G. Ron Austing

Except for the barred outer tail feathers, the Downy is a miniature edition of the Hairy Woodpecker. The name Downy is a suggestion that the species is less mature, therefore, smaller in stature, than the Hairy Woodpecker. It is a fairly common permanent resident throughout the park, but is much more common below 3,500 feet. Generally, it is a more confiding bird and will allow a much closer approach for observation than will the Hairy. Like most other woodpeckers, the Downy's tongue is very important in gathering food. The tongue is sticky and has a multibarbed tip. It can be extended well beyond the tip of the mandibles and worked, snake-like, into the burrows of boring insects.

The Downy is most conspicuous during the winter months when the trees are bare of their foliage. At this time it is frequently a member of foraging flocks of songbirds in the lower to middle elevations. The flocks often include Carolina Chickadees (whose call notes may first attract your attention), Tufted Titmice, nuthatches, and perhaps even a Brown Creeper and a kinglet or two. You can draw all the members of the flock in close by imitating the calls of an Eastern Screech-Owl.

HAIRY WOODPECKER

Picoides villosus
9¼ in (24 cm)

G. Ron Austing

Hairy Woodpeckers are fairly common permanent residents from the lowlands to the spruce-fir forests that crown the highest ridges. They are very similar in appearance to the smaller Downy Woodpecker, but are easily distinguished by the much larger, heavier bill. In general, the Hairy Woodpecker is much more common above 3,500 feet than it is below this elevation (the reverse is true of the Downy). It is the most frequently observed woodpecker in the Canadian zone forests. You will probably first become aware of its presence by its loud call note, a sharp *peek* or *pleek*. The noisy, buzzing sounds produced by the young of this and other woodpeckers may lead you to a nest tree in the late spring and summer.

The name *villosus* means "hairy or shaggy," which refers to the general appearance of the bird's plumage; an appearance that provides the common name as well. This is a big woodpecker, as large as the Red-bellied Woodpecker, which spends most of its time in dense, mature woodlands. Like many other woodpeckers, the Hairy's "song" is a drumming produced by repeatedly striking a dead limb or tree snag with its bill. During the breeding season such drumming plays an important role in the establishment of territory and the attraction of a mate.

Colaptes auratus
12½ in (32 cm)

Fred J. Alsop III

This is a fairly common permanent resident, but much more common from mid-March to October. The Northern Flicker frequents the edges of clearings and, though found at all elevations, is not often observed in Canadian zone forests. This woodpecker spends considerable time on the ground feeding on ants, one of its favorite foods. In spring and fall migration, small flocks of six to ten birds may be found. The yellow undersides of the wings and tail and the white rump patch are distinctive in flight. At close range the black "mustache" of the male can be seen. *Colaptes* is from the Greek for "chisel," an apt reference to "flicker" which means "one who strikes."

One of the best places to find the flicker is in the open country of Cades Cove. The flicker can be seen on the ground as it forages for food in the short-cropped grazed pastures. Watch for it also perched on the fence posts and sitting near the tops of trees. Flickers frequent the edges of woodlots and are rather conspicuous birds, often announcing their presence with a loud *klee-yerr* call. For many years I have seen flickers in the wind-topped snag of a sycamore tree that stands just on the east side of Hyatt Lane where it crosses Abrams Creek.

PILEATED WOODPECKER

Dryocopus pileatus
16½ in (42 cm)

G. Ron Austing

This, the largest woodpecker in the park, is a fairly common permanent resident. It is found throughout the Smokies, but is not as common in the spruce-fir forests. This almost crow-sized bird has a conspicuous red crest in both sexes and in all plumages. The bird can be easily missed because it spends most of its time within deep woodlands and may be silent for long periods. The call is loud and somewhat flicker-like, but with more resonance and fluctuation in loudness and pitch; like the sound of a Hollywood "jungle bird." The drumming, as befits its size, is the loudest of any woodpecker's in the area, and from a distance the bird's blows sound like a tree being struck with a wooden mallet. The bird often feeds close to the ground on stumps and fallen logs and you may flush it from the forest floor. It does not have the undulating flight so characteristic of other woodpeckers, but flies more like a crow with a steady wingbeat.

This woodpecker is the real life model for Woody Woodpecker of cartoon fame. Everything about the Pileated is impressive; its size, its movements, the loudness of its voice, the power it expresses as it chips away tree trunks with its heavy bill. What a woodpecker this is!

Contopus virens
6¼ in (16 cm)

EASTERN WOOD-PEWEE

J. Wedge/Vireo

The Eastern Wood-Pewee is a common summer resident at all elevations in the park, but is much more common below the belt of spruce and fir. The plaintive, clear whistled *pee-ah-wee, pee-err,* song of this little bird carries well and is at its best the first hour of dawn and again at dusk. Like other flycatchers, the pewee chooses a conspicuous perch from which to hawk insects, rest, preen, and sing. It often returns to the same vantage point after each hawking flight. The birds arrive in the park around the third week of April and are usually gone by late October. The pewee is easily separated from the previous species by the lack of tail-bobbing and, at close range, by its yellowish lower mandible that is distinctly different from the completely dark bill of the phoebe.

This is a bird of the forests and forest edges. It can be found in mature woodlands as well as secondary growth and younger successional forest stages.

ACADIAN FLYCATCHER

Empidonax virescens
5¾ in (15 cm)

G. Ron Austing

6	
5	
4	
3	
2	
1	
S	W	M

*E*mpidonax means "king of the gnats" and is a reference both to the small size of the birds and to the little flying insects they catch in midair. To the birder, *Empidonax* means a very difficult group of little greenish-gray flycatchers to identify. All have whitish wing bars and pale eye rings and are best identified by their distinctive voices, behavior, and preferred habitats. In late summer and during fall migration, when the birds rarely sing, few experts can reliably identify these species in the field. Five species in this genus have been recorded in the park and up to four of them may breed here.

The Acadian Flycatcher is probably the most common *Empidonax* here. It arrives about the third week in April and departs for its wintering grounds in Central America and northern South America by early October. Look for it along water courses and wet ravines bordered by rhododendron and hemlock below 3,500 feet. The best clue to its presence and identity is its voice. The explosive *peet-sa* sounds like a bird sneezing and can be heard from a good distance. The song appears to be given with such force that the bird's tail jerks upward and the body shakes with each utterance.

Sayornis phoebe
7 in (18 cm)

EASTERN PHOEBE

Fred J. Alsop III

This tail-bobbing flycatcher is a common permanent resident. It is the only flycatcher that spends the winter here, but it is much less common during the cold months when insects are difficult to find. It is found throughout the park, but is more common below 3,000 feet and is rarely found in the spruce-fir forests. Look for this bird along watercourses and around buildings. This is one species that has adapted well to man and his structures. Most Eastern Phoebe nests are now placed under the eaves of buildings, inside them, on window ledges, and under bridges and culverts. Almost any bridge below 4,000 feet elevation in the park probably has its pair of nesting phoebes in summer. There is usually a pair around the Sugarlands Visitor Center, and several nest in the reconstructed homesteads at Oconaluftee and Cades Cove. The bird says its name with a husky *fee-be*.

Between the third week of April and mid-October the only other species that you might confuse this bird with is the Eastern Wood-Pewee. But the pewee lacks the tail pumping behavior of the phoebe and has a yellowish lower mandible (unlike the dark mandibles of the phoebe) that is distinguishable at close range.

GREAT CRESTED FLYCATCHER

Myiarchus crinitus
8 in (20 cm)

G. Ron Austing

The Great Crested Flycatcher is a fairly common summer resident from the lowlands to the middle elevations. They are found chiefly in the broad-leaved forests. The birds spend much of their time in the tree tops and would be easily overlooked but for their loud, clear, whistled *wheeeep* calls that are given frequently throughout the day. "Great Crested" is an ambitious name, for neither the bird nor the crest is large. They arrive in the park in mid-April and are usually gone on their southward migration by late August. The birds nest in cavities and are known to top-off the finished nest with a shed snakeskin. Today this practice continues, but many man-made articles such as cellophane and wax paper are often substituted for the less abundant reptile skins. Why this flycatcher uses a snakeskin as a finishing touch is not known, but it must have a startling effect on squirrels or other would-be intruders.

The rusty wingtips and tail are good field marks. Look and listen for the species in open, mature forests, in clearings, and along woodland edges.

Tyrannus tyrannus
8½ in (22 cm)

EASTERN KINGBIRD

Fred J. Alsop III

This large flycatcher is a fairly common summer resident in the park. A bird of open areas, the "bee martin" as the locals know it, finds little suitable habitat in these forested mountains. It is much more common in the agricultural areas outside the park; Wear Cove north of the park is an excellent place to search for it. The single best place in the park is Cades Cove. As you drive the one-way loop road, watch for this kingbird with its blackish upperparts, white underparts, and distinctive white-tipped tail. Most likely perches will be low ones, including weed tops in the fields, dead exposed branches, and wire fences.

The bird lives up to its name of tyrant. Almost any large bird that crosses its territory is scolded and chased. Crows, vultures, hawks, and others come under diving attacks that may last for many minutes. The kingbird may even strike the bird a blow with its beak and has been reported to land on a large bird's back and pull out feathers.

Kingbirds choose conspicuous perches from which to survey their territory and to hawk flying insects that make up most of their summer diet.

N. ROUGH-WINGED SWALLOW

Stelgidopteryx serripennis
5¾ in (14.5 cm)

G. Ron Austing

This is a fairly common resident from the end of March to the first of September. It ranges over all elevations in the park and should be watched for wherever there is an open vista. The following locations are some of the places I have seen the bird with regularity: the Newfound Gap parking area, the parking area at Sugarlands Visitor Center, the large pond (sewage lagoon) to the left and just beyond the entrance to the Cades Cove Loop Road, and the parking area at the orientation shelter at the loop road entrance.

One site where there is a small colony and where the swallows have nested for years is under the stone and concrete bridge at the Townsend "Y" (at the junction of the Townsend entrance and the Little River roads). Watch for the birds flying low over the water, perched on the dead limbs of streamside trees, and up high on the powerline that crosses the stream on the west side of the bridge.

Look for the slightly notched tail and the dusky brown throat. The genus name, *Stelgidopteryx*, is Greek for "scraper-winged." This species has stiff recurved hooks on its first primary feathers and, hence, is rough-winged.

Hirundo rustica
6¾ in (17 cm)

BARN SWALLOW

Fred J. Alsop III

This beautiful swallow is a common summer resident. It prefers open fields for feeding and is thus restricted, generally, to a few low open areas in the park. It is very common in the agricultural areas surrounding the national park. Perhaps the two best places to find it are the Oconaluftee Visitor Center and Cades Cove. It places its mud nests on the rafters of barns and other buildings and sometimes under bridges and culverts. I have often watched two adult Barn Swallows seeming to play with a feather as it was being transported to the nest site. One bird would release a feather from its bill and then dive, pick it from midair, and repeat the performance over and over. Sometimes the swallow allowed the falling feather to be taken by another bird (the mate?). Barn Swallows nest as pairs or in small colonies.

It is easily recognized as the only swallow here with a deeply forked tail. The Barn Swallow is a strong, graceful flier and often feeds on flying insects only a few feet above the fields.

BLUE JAY

Cyanocitta cristata
11 in (28 cm)

T. Vezo/Vireo

The Blue Jay is a common permanent resident at all elevations in the park. It is big and noisy and the *jay, jay, jay,* or *thief, thief, thief* calls carry far. Flocks, sometimes numbering 50 or more birds, may be observed in spring and late fall. Blue Jays are mostly vegetarians and feed on beech-nuts and acorns. They often gather more of these nuts than they can eat, and their habit of burying the extras makes them a chief agent in the distribution and growth of oak and beech forests. Like their larger relatives, the crows, jays seem to delight in discovering a hawk or owl to mob with harsh, vocal protests. These noisy aggregations have often revealed the location of an Eastern Screech-Owl to me.

The jay's scientific name is descriptive; *Cyanocitta* is Greek for "blue jay" and *cristata* is Latin for "crested." The bright blues of the jay's feathers are caused by structural elements within the feather that reflect the blue wave lengths of light. The next time you find a Blue Jay feather, crush it between your finger and thumb and watch the blue color fade and disappear as you mechanically break down the feather's structure.

Corvus brachyrhynchos
17½ in (45 cm)

AMERICAN CROW

G. Ron Austing

The American Crow is a fairly common to common permanent resident that is most abundant in the lower altitudes during all seasons. Solitary birds and small groups can be seen along the Newfound Gap Road. Be careful not to confuse them with the larger, and much less common, Common Raven. Crows have a fan-shaped tail and a shorter, more slender bill.

Cades Cove is the one place in the park where you could almost be guaranteed of seeing one or more of these big black birds. There they are usually the most conspicuous form of wildlife, and the long years without being shot at have made them quite bold.

Crows are often seen in pairs or small flocks. Usually a group that is foraging on the ground seems to have at least one lookout and all retreat to safety when the alarm calls are given. During the winter the size of the flocks may be noticeably increased, perhaps by birds migrating from the north. In flight the wingbeats are deep and slow, almost as if the crow is rowing its way through the air.

COMMON RAVEN

Corvus corax
24 in (61 cm)

T. J. Ulrich/Vireo

This, the largest of our songbirds, may soar on ebony wings that span almost four feet. It is a fairly common permanent resident in the park. Ravens may occasionally be found in the lower elevations in winter, but the higher and more remote regions of the mountains are its familiar haunts. It is a living symbol of the wilderness, frequenting the craggy cliffs and the silent solitude of the spruce-fir forests. For many years there has been an active nest on the walls of Peregrine Peak, near Alum Cave, within binocular view of the trail. The high mountain road from Newfound Gap to Clingmans Dome is a good place to watch for them. I have seen ravens at Indian Gap many times.

Don't confuse them with the more abundant American Crow that may also be present along these roads. Look for the heavy bill and wedge-shaped tail that are characteristic of the Common Raven. Ravens often soar on outstretched wings riding the uplifting winds along the ridges and mountain crests. They, perhaps more than any other bird I know, seem to delight in their abilities of flight. I have watched them fall and tumble in the skies, stooping on one another, or on other large soaring birds, executing barrel rolls and loop-the-loops as if for the pure joy of it. Their harsh *cronk, cronk, cronk* calls can be heard over long distances above the stillness of the high spruce-fir forests.

Parus atricapillus BLACK-CAPPED CHICKADEE
5¼ in (13 cm)

G. Ron Austing

A fairly common permanent resident, the Black-capped Chickadee undertakes a vertical migration between the breeding and winter seasons. The species occurs mostly above 3,000 feet during the late spring and summer months, nesting chiefly above 4,000 feet. In winter most of the population moves down into the middle elevations and some into the lowlands. In plumage, general appearance, and behavior it is very much like the slightly smaller Carolina Chickadee, which is also common in the park. The best clue to identification is the voice; a whistled *fee-bee* or *fee-bee-ee* song different from the *fee-bee, fee-bu* of the Carolina. Almost any chickadee you find in the spruce-fir forests should be a Black-capped, but check it carefully.

The breeding season begins in late April and early May in the northern hardwood forests and in the spruce-fir forests above them. Listen for the calls and songs of the Black-capped Chickadee and watch for it in woodlands that contain yellow birch. These chickadees often choose standing, dead yellow birch for excavating their nesting cavities because of the relative softness of the wood. Cavities created by woodpeckers and other birds may also be used for nesting. Chickadees will often come to the squeaking sounds produced by loudly "kissing" the back of your hand or to the whistled imitation of a Northern Saw-whet Owl's song.

CAROLINA CHICKADEE

Parus carolinensis
4¾ in (12 cm)

Fred J. Alsop III

A common permanent resident in the middle and lower elevations of the park, it is usually found at altitudes below 4,000 feet. While this and the preceding species are similar in appearance and habits, there is a constant gap between the breeding ranges of the two species and hybridization takes place rarely, if ever. After the young are fledged, the family may stay together feeding in mixed flocks with titmice, warblers, nuthatches, and others. These extremely active little birds often feed while hanging beneath the tip of a branch or cone. They are inquisitive and will often come close if you make squeaking sounds on the back of your hand or, better, imitate the call of the Eastern Screech-Owl.

The Carolina Chickadee's call is a higher, thinner, and faster *chick-a-dee-dee-dee* than the Black-capped's and the voice is also different (see Black-capped Chickadee). Look for them in any of the southern woodlands in the park as well as in the wooded residential areas in communities adjacent to the park, including Gatlinburg and Cherokee.

Parus bicolor
6½ in (17 cm)

TUFTED TITMOUSE

G. Ron Austing

This small gray bird with its distinctive crest is a common permanent resident in broad-leaved forests primarily below 5,000 feet. It is most often seen in small flocks and its loud *peter, peter, peter* calls can be heard almost any day of the year. After the nesting season it may feed in loose flocks composed of several species. In these mixed flocks you may find several titmice in the company of Carolina Chickadees, White-breasted Nuthatches, Downy Woodpeckers, and, in late summer, a Black-and-white Warbler or two. In winter a kinglet, Yellow-rumped Warbler, and Brown Creeper might be added to the group. Like the chickadees, titmice respond to squeaking noises and to the imitated calls of the Eastern Screech-Owl. They will frequently make close approaches to such sounds. The Tufted Titmouse inhabits all the low elevation campgrounds and should be easily added to your trip list.

I learned this bird from my grandfather who called it a spring warbler. He was not the first to confuse the bird's identity. The common name, titmouse, has nothing to do with the grayish mousy color of the bird's plumage, but, rather, its etymological origins are steeped in Old Icelandic and Old English words for a "small bird."

RED-BREASTED NUTHATCH *Sitta canadensis*
4½ in (11 cm)

J. Wedge/ Vireo

The Red-breasted Nuthatch is a permanent resident in the park whose numbers fluctuate widely from year to year. It is found in the breeding season chiefly above 3,000 feet and normally can be found in the spruce-fir forests at this time. Listen for its small, *ank, ank, ank* vocalizations given with tin-horn quality. In winter the Red-breasted Nuthatch can be found at almost any elevation, but you will probably have better luck in stands containing hemlocks, pines, and other conifers whose seeds provide important food. In some winters it is uncommon to virtually absent, while in others it is abundant. The numbers present are apparently related to the success or failure of the seed crops of northern conifers.

These short-tailed little acrobatic birds share the abilities of the larger White-breasted Nuthatch of walking up, walking down, and walking around tree trunks and branches as they search for insects in the bark. They are equally at ease clinging upside down from a lofty evergreen cone as they work at extracting the seeds that are a mainstay in their diet. This is the most strikingly marked nuthatch in North America and reaches near the southern limits of its eastern breeding range in the Smokies.

WHITE-BREASTED NUTHATCH

Sitta carolinensis
5¾ in (15 cm)

G. Ron Austing

This is a fairly common permanent resident found primarily in the broad-leaved forests from just below the spruce and fir downward through the lowest elevations. Superficially, it resembles the more common chickadees in some of its behavior and plumage, but it lacks the black bib on the throat. Nuthatches are birds that seem to defy gravity. They are unique among North American birds in their ability to walk head-first down a vertical tree trunk. On branches, they walk in a spiraling manner that also brings them upside down. As they continue walking and feeding over the tree's surface, producing their distinctive nasal *yank yank*, they remind me of little wind-up toys and I almost expect to see a slowly turning key in the center of their backs.

Nuthatches nest in tree cavities which they may excavate themselves. The common name, nuthatch, is a corruption of *nuthack*, a description of some of the bird's feeding behavior. Nuthatches commonly open nuts and other large seeds by wedging them into the crevices of a tree's bark and then hacking them open with their bill. The genus name *Sitta* comes from the Greek for a bird that pecks on the bark of a tree in reference to this seed-opening habit.

BROWN CREEPER

Certhia americana
5¼ in (13 cm)

Fred J. Alsop III

The Brown Creeper is a fairly common permanent resident in the park. It generally breeds above 4,500 feet and is common in the spruce-fir in the spring, summer, and early fall months. Some birds apparently migrate downward to lower elevations as winter approaches and their numbers are swelled by creepers from further north migrating here. The most common nest site is a very unusual one. The nest is constructed against the trunk of a tree beneath a slab of overhanging bark. The bark not only acts to conceal the structure but serves to protect it from the elements. Beginning in the mid-1980s, I recorded Brown Creepers in late April, May, and early June in Cades Cove, elevation 1,800 feet. This was late enough in the year that birds may be breeding at lower elevations than previously observed. In Cades Cove during these months, look for the bird in the mixed pine and hardwoods along the horse trail to the sewage lagoon and in the "gum swamp" near the Cable Cemetery. During winter, look for this well camouflaged bird in any woodlot at any elevation.

Certhia is a Latinized form of a Greek word said to have been given by Aristotle to a tree-creeping bird. As you watch the feeding bird, the reasoning for its name becomes readily apparent. It hitches up the trunk in a series of climbing spirals and then drops to the base of another tree to repeat the process.

Thyrothorus ludovicianus
5½ in (14 cm)

CAROLINA WREN

G. Ron Austing

This wren is a common permanent resident below 3,000 feet, but its numbers may be much reduced following severe winters. It is found in deciduous woodlands, in tangles near clearings, and in the vicinity of buildings. Stream edges seem to be preferred habitat and you might work the margins to find this "reed-leaper" (the genus name alludes to the damper woodland haunts it may frequent). The bird has been recorded in the high elevations, including Clingmans Dome parking area, but is not to be expected there.

This, the largest and buffiest wren in the park, has a white eye stripe and a loud, ringing *teakettle teakettle teakettle* song that may be heard at any month of the year. The song of the male, or the long, drawn-out *chirrrrr* notes given by both sexes, are familiar sounds in these southern broad-leaved forests. Carolina Wrens are easily attracted to an observer by making squeaking noises on the back of one's hand or by the imitated (or recorded) calls of the Eastern Screech-Owl. The wren's calls will often attract other species curious to discover the source of the irritation. Look for this wren in any of the low elevations at any time of year, including Sugarlands, Cades Cove, Oconaluftee, and Cosby.

WINTER WREN

Troglodytes troglodytes
4 in (10 cm)

Dr. M. Stubblefield/Vireo

A common permanent resident in the park, the Winter Wren breeds in the high altitudes, especially the dark haunts of the spruce-fir forests. In winter a few remain in the high elevations, but most are in the middle to low levels of the park. It is one of the smallest songbirds in the Smokies and has the longest, and one of the loudest, songs. You can't mistake the musical series of bubbling warbles and trills that may last for five seconds or more. Antiphonal singing has been heard on rare occasions when, just as one singer gives his last note, the song is picked up by another singer, and then another, until the tune cascades up and down the mountain slopes for many minutes. Look for the short tail cocked over the back and the dark barred belly of this chunky little brown bird.

The Winter Wren's long energetic song is one of my favorite sounds of the high Canadian zone forests. In summer, walk out one of the many trails in the spruce-fir forests and find a comfortable, moss-draped log to sit on. These are silent forests, but as you sit quietly for a few minutes you will almost surely be rewarded by the rich smells of the conifers and the marvelously long, melodic song of the Winter Wren. One wonders in awe at the ability of such a small creature to produce such a loud and lengthy vocalization without seeming to want for a breath.

GOLDEN-CROWNED KINGLET

Regulus satrapa
4 in (10 cm)

G. Ron Austing

The Golden-crowned Kinglet is a common permanent resident in the spruce-fir forests where it breeds. It is also found in the lower altitudes from October to early April when wintering individuals from the north are probably joined by some of the park's residents from higher up the slopes. At these times, it is often in the company of chickadees, nuthatches, titmice, creepers, and others. Kinglets have the habit of flicking open their wings as they hop from perch to perch in the trees, a good clue to the bird's identity in poor light, and a bit of behavior that may startle a steadfast insect into a fatal twitch.

The Golden-crowned Kinglet is easily located in the spruce-fir forests. You should have little trouble finding the bird in the conifers along the road from just below Newfound Gap to Clingmans Dome. The small bird is difficult to see in the interiors of the conifers as these are rather dark forests. You will probably first locate the species by the frequent *tsee tsee tsee* notes, typically given in groups of threes. Kinglets are not overly shy birds and you should be able to follow their call notes to a position very close to the foraging birds.

Their nests are softball-sized, spherical structures covered with living green moss and attached near the tips of lofty branches of spruce or fir.

RUBY-CROWNED KINGLET *Regulus calendula*

4¼ in (11 cm)

G. Ron Austing

The Ruby-crowned Kinglet is a fairly common transient and winter resident. It can be found in all elevations in the park, but in winter it is more likely to be observed in the lower elevations. Look for it in the forests and forest edges, but particularly in stands of pine and hemlock. This kinglet is most abundant in October, March, and April. They are usually gone by early May. In summer it is often recorded as a solitary bird or with only one or two other individuals, but not in small conspecific flocks like the Golden-crowned Kinglet. The Ruby-crowned Kinglet does join in mixed foraging flocks of other small songbirds in the winter.

After finding and watching this species you may ask, where is the ruby crown? It is most assuredly there, but it is seldom visible. In March and April, when males sing their loud, long, and very melodious song, one is occasionally treated with a flash of the crown that makes the bird's head appear to be covered with bright blood! I have seen this quickly given display most often when a singing male was in close proximity of another kinglet of the same species. The white eye ring and lack of both striped crown and eye stripes easily distinguish this species from the similar sized Golden-crowned Kinglet.

BLUE-GRAY GNATCATCHER

Polioptila caerulea
4½ in (11 cm)

G. Ron Austing

This is a common summer resident in mixed and deciduous forests below 2,500 feet. It usually arrives here by the third week of March and is gone from the park by late September. The lispy *spee, spee, spee* call sounds like it's from a baby bird and is usually the first indication that the gnatcatcher is nearby. It feeds high in the trees, fluttering out near the tips of the branches, as it picks off insects. Its black tail with the white borders is often jerked from side to side or cocked, wren-like, over the back. In addition to the tail, the white eye ring is a good field mark. The nest often looks like a knot on a horizontal limb. It is a well-constructed cup covered with spider webs and lichens and often nosily attended by the adults. These birds usually nest near park headquarters at Sugarlands and should be easily found there in proper season.

Many people have their own harbingers of spring; in the northern states the American Robin's return is often the long-awaited signal. The Blue-gray Gnatcatcher has been my messenger of these coming events for the quarter century I have been birding.

EASTERN BLUEBIRD

Sialia sialis
7 in (18 cm)

G. Ron Austing

This thrush with the blue of the sky on its back is a fairly common, but local, permanent resident. It has been observed flying over the highest mountain top, but it nests below 5,000 feet, becoming much more common in the lower elevations. It is a bird that frequents the more open areas of the park, but it retires to woodlands in the winter. Look for it around Cades Cove and Oconaluftee. Common nesting sites are cavities in trees and fence posts. Severe winters with ice and snow storms which cover the berries of poison-ivy and sumac may cause many bluebirds to perish.

Bluebirds are usually found in pairs or small groups, particularly after the nesting season. These birds not only seek suitable cavities for their nesting, they also spend cold winter nights huddled together in a snug roosting hole which increases the chances for survival. Bluebirds will readily accept man-made nesting/roosting boxes constructed to proper dimensions and placed in open areas away from overhanging trees.

Catharus fuscescens
7 in (18 cm)

VEERY

G. Ron Austing

The Veery is a common summer resident above 3,500 feet in the park. It is found in the northern hardwood forests as well as the spruce-fir forests from late April through September. Its beautiful, downward-cascading, flute-like song is one of the sounds of the high mountains at sunset you are likely never to forget. The bird sings early in the day, but its best singing is done at dusk from late April through mid-July. It is one of the few species that may sing when fogs bathe the peaks. During spring and early summer, take time to hike far enough from the highway into the northern hardwood or spruce-fir forests so that you are beyond the sounds of traffic. If you have chosen a late afternoon or a period just following a summer shower, or if the fog is lifting, you may be serenaded by one of the outstanding songsters of the park. For me it has always been a journey well worth making.

Like the Wood Thrush, the Veery spends a great deal of time on the forest floor and can be difficult to locate. The entire upperparts are more rusty in color than other thrushes and the buffy breast is less spotted.

SWAINSON'S THRUSH

Catharus ustulatus
7 in (18 cm)

Fred J. Alsop III

6	
5	
4	
3	//
2	//
1	//
S W M	

This rather shy thrush is a common spring and fall migrant that seems to be somewhat more conspicuous here in the fall. It passes through these mountains from the last week of April to mid-May in its northward rush to its breeding grounds. Watch for this bird's southbound flight from early September through the third week of October. The distinct buffy eye ring, buffy lores, and spotted, buffy breast distinguish this from other spotted brown thrush species.

When Swainson's Thrushes are present, they are much more common in the lower elevations. I often first hear its common call note, a liquid *whit* that sounds like a bird's imitation of a falling drop of water. In their autumn migration these thrushes feed on berries and can be found in the company of robins, Veerys, and other thrushes foraging on the fruits of pokeberry, flowering dogwood, black cherry, and American mountain-ash. Locating one of these fruiting trees will frequently produce lengthy observations of this skittish bird.

Hylocichla mustelina
7¾ in (20 cm)

WOOD THRUSH

Fred J. Alsop III

This thrush is a common summer resident in the broad-leaved forests below 5,000 feet. The bird arrives in the park around the second week of April and departs in mid-October. Its lovely flute-like phrases roll from the woodlands throughout the day, but especially during the first hours of daylight and the last of the evening, from the day of its arrival into August. It spends much of its time on or just above the forest floor.

All the campgrounds in the low elevations have their summer Wood Thrushes. You should also find it on several of the short self-guiding nature trails such as Cosby, Sugarlands, Cove Hardwood, Cades Cove, and others. Some of the high trails in the northern hardwoods have both Wood Thrushes and Veerys and you may hear and see both in these areas of habitat overlap. One such place reached by a short walk is the Alum Cave Trail. Another place where I have always found the Wood Thrush is the Chimneys Picnic Area where the birds often feed on the ground near your tables.

AMERICAN ROBIN

Turdus migratorius
10 in (25 cm)

G. Ron Austing

The robin is a fairly common permanent resident found throughout the park. It is common on the lawns in the communities around the park, in the lowlands, and in the spruce-fir forests of the high ridges. It is present, but somewhat hard to find, in the middle altitudes. In the coniferous forests of the mountaintops this thrush seems wilder and less approachable than robins in the lowlands. From late August through mid-March robins may be encountered in flocks which sometimes number hundreds of birds. The familiar adults with their orange breasts are easily recognized. Juveniles' plumage shows that they are, indeed, thrushes with their spotted breasts (a dress they will lose in their next molt).

The American Robin is without doubt one of the most familiar birds in North America. Look for them on the lawns at Sugarlands or Oconaluftee visitor centers, in the short grassy pastures in Cades Cove, and at Clingmans Dome parking area and Newfound Gap. In fall and winter watch for foraging individuals and flocks in fruiting trees such as flowering dogwood, American holly, sumacs, and black gum.

Dumetella carolinensis
8½ in (22 cm)

GRAY CATBIRD

Fred J. Alsop III

This bird is a fairly common summer resident found at all altitudes, but it is more common at lower elevations. A few occasionally spend the winter in sheltered areas at the base of the mountains. Migrants begin arriving in the park in mid-April and leave in October. This bird is so closely associated with low, dense undergrowth that even its genus name *Dumetella*, from the Latin "little shrub or bush," makes note of its haunts. It occurs in the high elevations at edges of grass balds, on heath balds, in rhododendron and blackberry bushes, and in blow-downs in the forest. Catbirds respond readily to squeaking noises made on the back of your hand. A catlike, mewing scold is the common call that gives rise to the bird's name. It is a good singer and an excellent mimic.

This plain, dark gray, long-tailed bird is a mimic thrush in the same family as the Northern Mockingbird. Like the mockingbird, it is a good songster and the catbird's song is similar to the mockingbird's. However, unlike the mockingbird's, the catbird's song is continuous and without repetition. Listen long enough to the variable mixture of notes coming from the depths of the thicket and you will hear the distinctive, downslurred *mew* note that erases any doubt as to the identity of the hidden singer.

BROWN THRASHER

Toxostoma rufum
11½ in (29 cm)

J. Schumacher/Vireo

The Brown Thrasher is a fairly common summer resident that sometimes remains through the winter. This big brown thrush arrives around the first of March and remains well into October. Most of the breeding population ranges below 5,000 feet. This bird is distinguished by its long tail, long decurved bill, and heavily streaked breast. Thrashers spend much time on the ground and you may find them turning over leaves and digging into the soil with their bills for invertebrates. The song is similar to the Northern Mockingbird's, but the phrases are generally repeated only once. It, too, is a good mimic.

This large bird is most conspicuous when the males are singing on territory. In the lower elevations this activity begins in late March and continues into May. Singing males prefer a prominent perch and often sing from the very top of a tree making them easy to locate and observe. Brown Thrashers frequent woodland edges, overgrown fencerows, and brushy areas. They will often appear from their secluded perches in response to squeaking noises made on the back of your hand. I have often seen one run onto the road ahead of me with its long tail sticking straight out behind and looking for all the world like a miniature roadrunner.

Bombycilla cedrorum
7¼ in (18 cm)

CEDAR WAXWING

Fred J. Alsop III

Waxwings are a very erratic species. The park's population changes from fairly common during most of the year to common in the summer. They seem to prefer the lowlands of the park during the winter months, and the largest flocks are usually seen then. This is not a species that one goes out and searches for in the usual sense, for waxwings are wanderers and roam widely in search of fruits and berries. In summer you may find them more readily in the high elevations, especially along the edges of the spruce-fir forest and around the balds. Learning their call, a soft, high-pitched, trilled whistle, is one of the best ways to locate them.

The name "waxwing" is an allusion to the red tips of some of the secondary feathers of the wing which recalled to some long forgotten birder the color of sealing wax. Not all birds show the waxy tips and some have much more than others. The Cedar Waxwing is one of the few crested species in the park and the only one with a yellow-tipped tail. Waxwings feed on the berries produced by many plants in the park, including pokeberry, American mistletoe, flowering dogwood, American mountain ash, American holly, poison ivy, serviceberry, pin cherry, and black cherry. In early spring the birds may descend on the greening buds of many deciduous trees, including elm.

EUROPEAN STARLING

Sturnus vulgaris
8½ in (22 cm)

G. Ron Austing

This species, introduced from Europe in the late 1800s, is one of the few non-native species of birds that occurs in the park. It is a permanent resident that is more common in the suburban and agricultural areas surrounding the park. Look for this dark, glossy, chunky bird with the yellow bill (brownish in winter) in open, grassy areas in the low elevations; places like Oconaluftee Pioneer Farmstead, Elkmont, and especially Cades Cove. In late summer and winter the starling often occurs in large flocks.

Starlings are aggressive birds. Nest-seeking individuals often outcompete native species like bluebirds and woodpeckers for nesting holes. Starlings are so successful at claiming nesting chambers that in some areas other hole nesting species may decline in numbers. Even larger birds like Pileated Woodpeckers are not immune to the onslaught of nest-seeking starlings.

The European Starling is an accomplished songster and often includes the songs of other birds in its repertoire. It is particularly good at imitating the Eastern Wood-pewee and the Northern Bobwhite.

Vireo griseus
5 in (13 cm)

WHITE-EYED VIREO

Fred J. Alsop III

The White-eyed Vireo is a fairly common summer resident below 3,000 feet. It arrives here around the first week of April and is usually gone by the end of September. On its breeding grounds it is a bird of thickets and old fields. Look for it and listen for the *quick-with-the-beer-check* song from the tangles of blackberries and low shrubs and in the borders between field and forest. It is common in the agricultural areas outside the park boundaries. The white iris of the eye may be seen in adults at close range. Unlike other species of vireos, the nest of the White-eyed Vireo is usually within six feet of the ground.

Perhaps one of the best places to search for this vireo in the park is in Cades Cove where Hyatt Lane crosses Abrams Creek. There are weedy tangles along the creek and a pair or two of these birds are usually summer residents here. The oxbow area of the same creek just upstream from the road going to the Abrams Falls parking area is bordered by willows and blackberry tangles that may also produce this species in proper season. This little vireo boldly defends his nesting territory and will make close, scolding approaches if you make squeaking noises on the back of your hand.

BLUE-HEADED VIREO

Vireo solitarius
5½ in (14 cm)

B. Henry/Vireo

The Blue-headed Vireo is a common summer resident from the highest altitudes down to around 2,000 feet (in the lower elevations it is usually associated with hemlock stands). It is the first vireo to arrive in the spring (mid-March) and the last to leave in the fall (late October). This is the only vireo you are likely to encounter in the spruce-fir forests. The white spectacles of the eye ring and the lore contrasting against the slate gray head are good field marks. Places where the bird can usually be found in the proper season include: Chimneys Picnic Area, hemlock groves on the Roaring Fork Motor Nature Trail, Alum Cave Trail, and all of the spruce-fir forest. Vireo is from the Latin, "to be green," and most species have a touch of green in their plumage.

Blue-headed, Red-eyed, and Yellow-throated vireos all have a similar song pattern, a series of phrases and pauses. The mnemonics (word phrases) *look up . . . , see me . . . , over here . . . , higher. . .* and so on, may serve to describe the song. Learn the basic song of these three vireos and then listen for the subtle differences between the species: the Blue-headed is higher and sweeter with longer pauses than the Red-eyed Vireo. The Yellow-throated has slightly longer pauses than the Red-eyed, but sounds burrier, like he is singing with a sore throat.

Vireo flavifrons
5½ in (14 cm)

YELLOW-THROATED VIREO

```
6 _____
5 _____
4 _____
3 _____
2 ///_____
1 ///_____
  S  W  M
```

R. & N. Bowers/Vireo

This vireo, with distinctive yellow throat and breast, is a common summer resident of the deciduous forests below 3,000 feet. It usually arrives around the end of the first week of April and leaves in early October. The feeding actions of this and other vireos are slow and deliberate, very different from the slightly smaller, more active warblers they resemble. I usually find a pair of these birds in the trees around the park headquarters at Sugarlands. Look for them in the tall trees around the lawn and in the trees around the employee parking lot behind this building. These vireos are birds of the treetops and are often discovered upon hearing their loud, distinctive song. The song is similar to the more common Red-eyed Vireo's, but huskier, like a Red-eyed with a sore throat.

Cades Cove has always been a good place to find Yellow-throated Vireos in the spring and summer. Look and listen around the campground store and along the tree border of Abrams Creek where Sparks Lane and Hyatt Lane cross it. On Sparks Lane, watch for nesting Yellow-throated Vireos in the large cherry trees along both sides of this pleasant country road.

RED-EYED VIREO

Vireo olivaceus
6 in (15 cm)

G. Ron Austing

This bird is a common to abundant summer resident in broad-leaved forests chiefly below 4,500 feet. A persistent singer, the voice of this woodland species may be heard from dawn to dusk during summer from almost any suitable habitat in the park. (See Solitary Vireo for song description.) The red eye, though distinctive, is not as good a field mark as the prominent eye stripe and lack of wing bars. The birds spend much of their day high in the forest canopy and you may have to crane your neck skyward to find a singing male as he sits almost motionless while giving his endless phrases. The "preacher" is perhaps one of the most common birds in the woodlots of Eastern North America, and you should have little trouble locating it between the middle of April and early October in the park.

As common as the Red-eyed Vireo is today, it was probably even more abundant when this country's forests were still largely untouched by man. It seems to require trees in its summer range and so its populations must be greatly reduced. The species continues to suffer a loss of habitat not only in this country, but also in the South American countries where it winters, and where significant deforestation continues. Still, it remains a common species in the park, and one any visitor with a little effort and modest birding skills can locate.

Parula americana
4½ in (11 cm)

NORTHERN PARULA

G. Ron Austing

The Northern Parula is a fairly common summer resident from the lowlands to approximately 5,200 feet. Parulas arrive in the first week of April and stay in the park until the first of October. They live in wooded areas and are more frequent where the trees border streams. Look for parulas in the small "gum swamp" to the left (north) of the Cades Cove Loop Road a few hundred yards east of the Becky Cable cemetery. The junction of Mill Creek and Abrams Creek near the Abrams Falls parking area (also in Cades Cove) is another good spot. One additional location is the park headquarters and visitor center area at Sugarlands. The low, wet, wooded area just north of the west end of the Sugarlands Visitor Center parking area often has nesting Northern Parula warblers. If you fail to find the bird there, search the sweetgums adjacent to the visitor center and the trees around the parking area behind the stone head-quarters building.

This is a tiny warbler, the smallest that occurs in the park, and it is often revealed by the male's song, a buzzy, rising trill ending in a lower *zip* note. The typical song always reminds me of the sound of a cup being filled with water and suddenly spilling over. It sings with its head thrown back and with its body trembling all over with the effort. Look for it in the tree tops and near the tips of the branches.

YELLOW WARBLER

Dendrocia petechia
5 in (13 cm)

Fred J. Alsop III

The Yellow Warbler is a fairly common summer resident in open areas below 3,000 feet, particularly in willows and low shrubby vegetation and along streams. The birds begin to arrive on their breeding grounds in the first week of April and the clear, musical *sweet, sweet, sweet, I'm so sweet* song of the males can be heard in the park as well as in Cherokee and Gatlinburg. The warbler begins its fall migration to wintering grounds in Mexico and Central and South America early, for most are gone from the park by the second week of August.

In most years a pair can be located on the grounds around the Sugarlands Visitor Center and I have found their nest in the last week of April in the small trees next to the building's north (back) wall. This is one bird with a truly descriptive name, for the Yellow Warbler is one of the few North American birds that appears all yellow in the field. The species name, *petechia*, is Latin for "having red spots on the skin" and is in reference to the red streaks on the breast of the male.

CHESTNUT-SIDED WARBLER

Dendroica pensylvanica
5 in (13 cm)

Fred J. Alsop III

This warbler is a common summer resident from the highest elevations down to approximately 3,000 feet. It arrives here around the middle of April and departs in mid-October. Look for this handsome warbler in brushy places where there is an opening in the forest canopy. It is a bird that relies on some disturbance, natural or man-made, to create the scrubby, second-growth environment it requires for its breeding territory. Landslides, fire, blow-downs, lumbering, tree diseases, road construction, and other forces that cause breaks in the forest create proper habitat for this warbler. Watch for it in the blackberry tangles along the Newfound Gap Road and in the heath balds of rhododendron. The wide chestnut stripe on this bird's side and the bright yellow cap are key field marks.

Spring comes "late" to the higher elevations, and the peak of this bird's nesting activity does not occur until mid-June. At this time it seems that every suitably sized patch of blackberry or rhododendron has its nesting pair of these beautiful warblers. Males are frequent singers before they begin to help feed their nestlings, and sometimes then a whispered version of their *please, please, pleased to meetcha* song can be heard. Some sing even when carrying a large green caterpillar to the nest. Other warblers which breed in the high elevations of the park are the Blackburnian, Black-throated Green, Black-throated Blue, and Canada.

BLACK-THROATED BLUE WARBLER

Dendroica caerulescens
5¼ in (13 cm)

N. Barnes/Vireo

Black-throated Blue is a most descriptive name for the adult males of this species. It is a common summer resident above 2,800 feet, arriving here in the middle of April and departing around the end of October. Driving the Newfound Gap Road from the Sugarlands Visitor Center you will hear the first slow, husky notes of this warbler's song at the Chimneys Picnic Area. A short walk during the breeding season along the Cove Hardwood Nature Trail should produce the species. Continue up the road and you will find the warbler at almost any stop all the way to Clingmans Dome. The nests are often placed low in the tangles of rhododendron, good places to stop and watch for this most attractive bird.

The Black-throated Blue is found both in the northern hardwood forests and in the spruce-fir. Look for it in the lower to middle areas of the trees, often on the larger interior branches. The female is distinctive with her white eyebrow line and squarish, white patch on her folded wing. The females of the Appalachian race that breed in the park have much grayer plumage than those of the more northern races shown in popular field guides. The loud *I am laz-zzzy* song makes males easy to locate.

YELLOW-RUMPED (MYRTLE) WARBLER

Dendroica coronata
5½ in (14 cm)

Fred J. Alsop III

This is the only warbler to be found in any numbers in the park during the winter. Then it is fairly common to abundant, especially in the lowland limestone areas where red cedars grow. It is absent from the highest altitudes in mid-winter. Birds begin to arrive here from their northern nesting grounds in late September and remain into May. They often forage in small mixed flocks with other species, feeding on insects, the fruits of poison ivy and red cedar, and other seeds and berries. We see them most often in their brownish fall plumage, except for the last few weeks here in spring when many are in their breeding dress. The bright yellow rump is a good field mark in any plumage and at any season. *Coronata* is from the Latin for "crowned" and it describes the yellow spot in the center of the crown of nuptial plumage adults.

Look for the Yellow-rumped (Myrtle) Warbler in the forest edges and in the brushy tangles along streams, especially in more open areas such as Cades Cove. The loud, flat *check* note is distinctive and often the first notice that the Yellow-rumped is nearby. The winter fruits of poison ivy seem to be a staple food and any stand of trees with the thick, hairy vines of this plant laced about them are good places to seek this warbler.

BLACK-THROATED GREEN WARBLER

Dendroica virens
5 in (13 cm)

Fred J. Alsop III

This common summer resident is perhaps the most widespread breeding warbler in the park. It occurs at all elevations from the spruce-fir covered peaks to the hemlock lined ravines. The bright yellow cheeks are a good field mark, but learn the *zee, zee, zee, zoo, zay* song, for you will hear many more of these than you will see. In late April and early May it is one of the most common bird sounds you will hear. The first birds arrive in late March and leave during the last of October. In the lower elevations, hemlocks seem to hold a special attraction for this species. Nests are usually high up in the trees, often 30 feet or more, and back from the tips of the branches.

The Black-throated Green Warbler is a bird of the forests. It often forages near the tips of the branches and seems to prefer evergreen trees. It is an active warbler when searching for insect food and you will frequently see it fly out from the branch tips and hawk an insect in mid-air, flycatcher fashion. If you only find one species of warbler in the Smokies during your summer visit, chances are it will be this one.

Dendroica fusca
5 in (13 cm)

BLACKBURNIAN WARBLER

G. Ron Austing

This warbler is a fairly common to common summer resident from the second week of April through the middle of October. It frequents forested areas from the spruce-fir down to about 3,000 feet. Within the park this species is most common in the spruce-fir forests of the high ridges. The bright orange throat and head markings seem to glow like embers in sharp contrast with the dark evergreen backdrop of the forest. Feeding, singing, and nesting are generally carried out high in the treetops. A short stop at almost any of the roadside pull-offs and overlooks from Clingmans Dome to Newfound Gap should produce this colorful species, especially if you are familiar with its thin, high-pitched song. Because the song is of such high frequency, the warbler is often overlooked on its breeding grounds and is probably perceived to be less common in the park than it actually is.

This is one of my favorite warblers because of its beauty and its haunts in the Smokies. What can be more breathtaking than a clear view of a singing male, seeming to be wearing a throat of flame and surrounded by the deep greens of a red spruce or Fraser fir? To my eye the flash of that bright orange throat and head is as striking as the ruby throat of a hummingbird.

YELLOW-THROATED WARBLER

Dendroica dominica
5½ in (14 cm)

G. Ron Austing

This bird is often called the "sycamore warbler" by local birders and is a fairly common summer resident below 2,500 feet. Most of the Yellow-throated Warblers in the park are associated with pine stands, but in many localities it nests in sycamores and other bottomland trees. It arrives here by the third week of March and has usually departed by the end of September. The birds generally stay in the treetops, but when they drop lower they often work along the larger limbs in the interior of the tree.

I have often seen breeding birds on the pine ridges just north of the Townsend "Y" (junction of the Townsend entrance and Little River roads) and near where the Cades Cove Loop Road crosses Abrams Creek in the west end of the cove. Generally, a breeding pair is present in the large trees immediately behind the park headquarters building in Sugarlands or in the large white pines nearer the visitor center. Territorial males are persistent singers and often choose an exposed perch in a pine to deliver their song. This behavior, coupled with their frequent, deliberate foraging on the larger interior branches, makes the Yellow-throated Warbler relatively easy to observe. The pine stands in the Metcalf Bottoms Picnic Area are also good areas to look for this warbler.

Dendroica palmarum
5½ in (14 cm)

PALM WARBLER

Dr. M. Stubblefield/Vireo

The Palm Warbler is a fairly common spring and fall migrant and an occasional to rare winter visitor in the park. Spring migrants are usually present from mid-April to mid-May and fall transients are found from early September well into October. Transients are sometimes observed in the higher elevations, but are most often encountered below 3,000 feet. All the winter records have been from the low elevations.

Look for this tail-wagging warbler in woodland borders, brushy areas, the open fields around Oconaluftee and Cades Cove, and on the lawns of areas like the Sugarlands Visitor Center. In late September and early October the Palm Warbler is sometimes very common and seen in large flocks of over 100 individuals. The bird often searches for food on the ground or close to it. I have seen numerous Palm Warblers in the row of trees bordering the sewage lagoon in Cades Cove. The rufous cap, streaked underparts, and constant wagging of the tail serve to identify this warbler.

Palm Warbler, from the Latin, *palmarum*, "of the palms" is a reference to this bird's tree of choice in its wintering range from South Carolina to Florida and westward along the Gulf Coast into Mexico and islands of the Caribbean.

BLACK-AND-WHITE WARBLER

Mniotilta varia
5¼ in (13 cm)

G. Ron Austing

This little zebra-striped bird is a common summer resident below 5,000 feet. It arrives around the end of March and departs in early October. A bird of the forest, the Black-and-white Warbler stays in close to the tree trunk and works along the main branches like a nuthatch or creeper when feeding. Though most of its life is spent well above the forest floor, the species begins life in a nest expertly hidden on the ground. After the nesting season you may find Black-and-whites in the company of other warbler species, and in loose flocks with chickadees, titmice, nuthatches, and others.

You may first detect this warbler by its high, thin *wee-see, wee-see, wee-sa* song. The genus *Mniotilta* is from the Greek for "moss plucker" and perhaps is a reference to its habit of foraging for insects among the mosses growing on trees. Only the adult male has the black cheeks.

Setophaga ruticilla
5¼ in (13 cm)

AMERICAN REDSTART

G. Ron Austing

This beautiful and active warbler is a fairly common summer resident in the second-growth hardwoods and woodland edges at elevations below 2,500 feet. The redstart arrives around the second week of April and departs for its southern wintering grounds by the third week of October.

Adult males are unmistakable, black-bodied warblers with large patches of orange on their sides, wings, and tail. Their bellies and undertail coverts are white. In addition to the active foraging and flitting common to many warbler species, redstarts hawk for insects in mid-air. When perched, redstarts habitually droop their wings and fan their tails, revealing the colorful patches of feathers.

The American Redstart is a bird of the deciduous woodlands, but look for it in woodland edges and breaks such as those created by roadways. Try Cherokee Orchard, the three overlooks around Maloney Point on the Little River Road 3.5 miles west of Sugarlands Visitor Center, and the Campbell Overlook on the Newfound Gap Road two miles south of Sugarlands. Look for the warbler in trees heavily draped with wild grape vines. If you learn the thin, high-pitched sibilant song, *zeet, zeet, zeet, zeet, ZEET*, with the last note louder and more explosive, you will locate the birds more easily.

WORM-EATING WARBLER

Helmitheros vermivorus
5¼ in (13 cm)

Fred J. Alsop III

The Worm-eating Warbler is a fairly common summer resident on
forested slopes below 3,000 feet. The bird arrives around the third week
of April and leaves during the middle of September. It is somewhat similar
in appearance to the much rarer and very local Swainson's Warbler, but is
buffier, lacks the rusty cap of the former, and has a central crownstripe. It
is a bird that spends a great deal of time on the ground in addition to
nesting there. Look for it on wooded slopes that have some brushy
undergrowth and groundcover. Young woods seem to be preferred to more
mature stands. The bird is more easily heard than seen and you should be
alert for any Chipping Sparrow-like song coming from the forest.

There are several locations near the Sugarlands Visitor Center that
often produce the species, particularly in April, May, and June. The
nearest to the visitor center is the old road behind the trailer dumping
station. Two good trails for this species are the Laurel Falls Trail and the
Huskey Gap Trail. I once found a nest with four eggs only a few inches
above the Huskey Gap Trail when the incubating female scurried out from
the ground nest as I walked by. She looked more like a mouse than a bird,
dragging both wings on the ground in an effort to lure my attention from
the nest site.

Seiurus aurocapillus
6 in (15 cm)

OVENBIRD

G. Ron Austing

The Ovenbird is a common summer resident in woodlands below 5,000 feet. It can be found here from the second week of April through the third week of October. It looks much like a miniature thrush as it walks over the leaf litter, but the Ovenbird has a much thinner bill and an orange crown patch.

The shape of the nest gives the Ovenbird its name. It is placed on the ground with an arched top, something like a small, leafy Dutch oven. Birders from the North will at once notice that our Ovenbirds don't sing like their Ovenbirds. Unlike the two-note phrases of *teacher-teacher* . . . commonly heard in northern states, the birds here give a single note, *teach, teach, teach*.

The singing of one territorial Ovenbird often stimulates the adjacent territory holder to proclaim his presence, which induces a third male to announce that he is still on station, which may cause other males to follow suit or hand the challenge back to the original singer. One of the best places to hear several Ovenbirds in such a vocal domino pattern is Cherokee Orchard. Check the Rainbow Falls parking area or the next one a few hundred yards east. Look for Ovenbirds on the ground, walking and singing on the forest floor, or on low perches just above it.

LOUISIANA WATERTHRUSH *Seiurus motacilla*
6 in (15 cm)

Fred J. Alsop III

This is a common summer resident along streams below 3,500 feet. It returns in the third week of March and remains through September. It is often seen flying just above a stream, or walking along the shore with its characteristic bobbing motion. You may locate one by its loud song, or just pick a pleasant stretch of mountain brook in the lower elevations and relax on a moss-covered rock. The waterthrush will be along.

Fighting Creek, behind the Sugarlands headquarters building, is a good place to look for this species. Stand on the bridge and scan the stream in both directions and you should have a waterthrush in a short while. Also, the drive along the Little River from the Elkmont turnoff to the Townsend "Y" should produce a dozen or more waterthrushes from late March to early June. Close inspection of this warbler will reveal the unspotted white throat, a fieldmark that helps to separate it from the similar Northern Waterthrush (*S. noveboracensis*), a migrant in the park. Now that you have taken time to find your waterthrush, spend some time observing it. It is truly a fascinating bird to watch and the streamside habitat only serves to enhance its charm.

Oporornis formosus
5¼ in (13 cm)

KENTUCKY WARBLER

Fred J. Alsop III

The Kentucky Warbler is a fairly common to common summer resident in deciduous woodlands below 3,500 feet. It arrives in the park around the third week of April and departs around the third week of September. It is a bird of deep dark forests and prefers the moister slopes and ravines. Much of its time is spent on or close to the ground and the nest is placed on the forest floor. Look for it in the ravines and riparian bottoms that have dense stands of herbaceous plants and vines on the forest floor (I have found nests in stands of poison ivy). Learn the song, for you will hear dozens for every one you see. The bird is a persistent singer and the *tur-dle, tur-dle,* or *churree, churree* notes are loud and carry far.

You can usually find several territorial pairs in the woodlands surrounding the Sugarlands Visitor Center (see "The Birder's Dozen"). Kentucky Warblers often respond well to squeaking noises made by sucking on the back of your hand or to the whistled imitation of an Eastern Screech-Owl's call.

As a native Kentuckian, I have always had a soft spot in my heart for this sleek-looking warbler with the black "sideburns" so favored by my teenage classmates in northern Kentucky. *Formosus* is Latin for "beautiful" and bespeaks the cleancut lines of the bird, its bold behavior and loud song, as well as the hues of its coat.

COMMON YELLOWTHROAT *Geothlypis trichas*
5 in (13 cm)

G. Ron Austing

This is a fairly common summer resident that can be found at all elevations. In the higher altitudes it is associated with streams bordered with deciduous shrubs, especially where the forest has large clearings. In the lowlands look for it in scrubby fields, brushy fence rows and tangles, and along streams. The bird arrives here around mid-April and departs in the last weeks of October. The wide black mask easily distinguishes the male. Look for it on the high elevation balds, Cades Cove, and around the Oconaluftee Visitor Center. It is common in the agricultural areas surrounding the park.

Yellowthroats are inquisitive and often respond to squeaking sounds made on the back of one's hand. Listen for their answer, a husky, *tchep* note from the interior of a thicket. If you keep up the disturbance, the masked bird will frequently work its way up for a better view, chipping all the while. Males sing often during the breeding season and their *witchy, witchy, witchy, witch* song carries far. Female yellowthroats are one of those birds that seem to lack any distinguishing field marks. They are olive above and yellowish below without the mask of the male.

Wilsonia citrina
5¼ in (13 cm)

HOODED WARBLER

Fred J. Alsop III

The Hooded Warbler is a common summer resident in woodlands generally below 4,000 feet. It arrives in the park around the second week of April and departs in late October. It not only sings persistently, but sings into the late summer and even during fall migration. It prefers woodlands with abundant undergrowth, especially those that include ravines or brushy stream borders. Most of this warbler's activity is within 15 feet of the ground. It often flicks its tail open revealing large white spots as it moves about. Several can usually be found in the woodlands surrounding Sugarlands Visitor Center. *Citrina*, from the Latin for "lemon," refers to the bright yellow underparts and face of this distinctive warbler.

The woodlands surrounding the Cades Cove Loop Road are especially good areas to look and listen for Hooded Warblers. I have often recorded the species near Campbell Overlook on the Newfound Gap Road, in the Cherokee Orchard area, and in the woodlands around the Oconaluftee Visitor Center. Ravines with good stands of rhododendron and small streams coursing through them seem to be favorite nesting sites. Hooded Warblers will often respond to the squeaking sounds made by "kissing" the back of your hand or the whistled imitation of a screech-owl.

CANADA WARBLER

Wilsonia canadensis
5¼ in (13 cm)

Fred J. Alsop III

This is a common summer resident from the highest altitudes to about 3,400 feet. It is present in the park from the last week of April through the middle of September. It is a bird of dark, shady tangles of shrubs. Canada Warblers seem to prefer rhododendron in moist situations, especially along streams. It is an inquisitive species and will often reveal itself to your squeaking sounds. Most clumps of rhododendron in the higher elevations have one or more pairs and you should find the bird with little effort. I have always found them along the first mile of the Alum Cave Trail and at the first pull-off on the North Carolina side just below Newfound Gap. Like many other birds in the high altitude forests of the Smokies, Canada Warblers will often allow a close approach, especially if your movements are stealthful.

The Canada Warbler may be one of the species to benefit from the current loss of mature spruce and fir trees in the high elevations. As the trees die or are blown down, the forest floor is opened up to more sunlight which promotes the growth of rhododendron. Bird counts I conducted on Mount Guyot in the late 1960s, prior to the death of these trees, and again in the mid-1980s, after the insect infestation, found more Canada Warblers living in the disturbed areas than had been present before.

Icteria virens
7½ in (19 cm)

YELLOW-BREASTED CHAT

Fred J. Alsop III

The chat is the largest of our warblers and is a fairly common summer resident from the low elevations up to 5,000 feet. It is most common at the lower elevations. This bird arrives around the third week of April and leaves the park in the first week of October. It is a bird of the thickets and you will find it where there are open areas in which low brush and weedy tangles of blackberry abound.

The chat is often hard to see as it slips through the brambles, but it is easy to hear. It sings often with a song composed of caws, squeaks, whistles, mews, cackles, and grunts; none of which is very musical. The song is usually delivered from out of sight inside a tree or thicket. Sometimes it's given in a display flight during the breeding season as the bird flies slowly with wings held high over his back and with his feet dangling beneath. As if to improve its song with practice, the chat often sings at night. Abrams Creek in Cades Cove is one of the best places to look for this bird in the park. It is a common bird in the old fields in the more settled areas outside the park.

Old, abandoned fields are good locations to search, especially if they have clumps of blackberry, flowering dogwood, sumac, or red cedar for singing perches. Many such former habitats within the park have slowly and naturally given way to the regrowth of the Eastern forest.

SUMMER TANAGER

Piranga rubra
7¾ in (20 cm)

G. Ron Austing

Summer Tanagers are fairly common to common summer residents in the lower elevations, primarily below 2,000 feet. They arrive sometime around the third week of April and are gone from the park by the middle of October. Mature woodlands, especially those of pine, oak, and hickory, are the best places to find the rosy red males and yellow-orange females. Robin-like songs coming from within the woodland should be investigated. The distinctive *picka-tucka-tuck* notes are the common calls of both males and females and are given throughout the summer. Cades Cove, Cherokee Orchard, and Sugarlands Visitor Center are good places to look.

The Summer Tanager remains a bright rosy red all year and many of the older residents of the region refer to it as "the summer red bird" to distinguish it from the cardinal, a permanent resident. Young males may be almost golden-orange in late summer and fall. Flying insects make up a considerable part of this tanager's diet and they are expert at hawking insects in mid-air. This bird also frequently tears open the nests of wasps to extract the larvae and pupae. Summer Tanagers seem to be partial to oak trees as nesting sites in the park.

Tanagers are birds of the treetops and they often forage and sing from high in the forest canopy.

Piranga olivacea
7 in (18 cm)

SCARLET TANAGER

G. Ron Austing

This "tropical" bird is a common summer resident of the forested regions below 5,000 feet. It arrives in the park around the third week of April and departs by the middle of October. In the breeding season there appears to be an altitudinal line of separation between this species and the closely related Summer Tanager. The Summer Tanager is seldom found above 1,500–2,000 feet, while the Scarlet Tanager is rarely found below 2,000 feet. Look for the bird in mature woods. It does most of its feeding in the treetops and, unless you are familiar with its song or distinctive call notes, it is easily overlooked despite the bright scarlet plumage of the adult male.

The song consists of four or five raspy notes similar in quality to that of the American Robin, but much shorter and burrier, like a robin with a sore throat. Preferred habitat seems to be slopes and ridges with stands of mixed pine and oaks, but it is found elsewhere.

When Scarlet Tanagers arrive, most of the trees are not yet in full foliage, and a Scarlet Tanager in a tree stands out like a glowing ornament. In late summer and fall migration, look for tanagers in fruit-bearing trees like flowering dogwood and black cherry where they compete with thrushes and waxwings for the fare.

NORTHERN CARDINAL

Cardinalis cardinalis
8¾ in (22 cm)

6	
5	
4	
3	
2	
1	
S W M	

G. Bailey/Vireo

This handsome, crested, large-billed bird is a common permanent resident in a variety of habitats, chiefly below 3,500 feet. You may find it in woodlands, at the edge of the forest where it borders streams or fields, along the roadside, in tangles and thickets, and in residential areas bordering the park. The bird is a strong singer and the rich, whistled phrases carry a long distance (the female sometimes sings in addition to the male, a most unusual situation in North American songbirds).

Cardinals sing most of the year, beginning on sunny days in January and continuing until they molt in August, after which singing is still heard infrequently. The male often sings from a conspicuous perch, making it easy to observe. The Latin name means "important" and the cardinals of the church are the senior and most important bishops in their red robes.

The large conical bill is used to crack open wild seeds and fruits, but the cardinal supplements its diet with insects in the warmer months. Its fondness for sunflower seeds makes it a regular visitor to backyard feeding stations and may help to explain the species' range expansion in the northeast and southwestern states in this century. Cardinals do much of their foraging on the ground or near it in the vegetation.

ROSE-BREASTED GROSBEAK

Pheucticus ludovicianus
8 in (20 cm)

J. Heidecker/Vireo

Males of this species are easily recognized as the only black and white birds in the park with rose-red breasts. Females look like large sparrows, but are distinguished by their large bills. Though these birds can be found almost throughout the park during migration, they are fairly common summer residents between 3,200 and 5,000 feet in the northern hardwood forests. The Rose-breasted Grosbeak arrives in mid-April and is usually gone from the area by late October. Rhododendrons seem to be a favorite nesting place, especially if they are along an edge or break in the forest canopy. Males often share the incubation duties and have been known to softly sing their robin-like song from the nest while covering the eggs.

Two good trails to try your luck for Rose-breasted Grosbeaks during the breeding season are the Chimney Tops Trail and the Alum Cave Trail, both easily reached from the Newfound Gap Road on the Tennessee side of the park. Territorial birds are usually singing from the understory here in May and June. Perhaps the best places to search for the bird is where there are mature trees along trails, streams, and roadways. Grosbeaks usually forage from midway up in the understory well into the treetops. In fall migration, watch for the birds in fruit-bearing trees such as flowering dogwood, black cherry, sumac, and American mountain-ash.

INDIGO BUNTING

Passerina cyanea
5½ in (14 cm)

G. Ron Austing

6	
5	
4	
3	
2	
1	
S W M	

This bunting is a common to abundant summer resident chiefly below 5,000 feet and an individual bird may stay, though rarely, through the winter. Most Indigo Buntings arrive here in the third week of April and remain well into October before departing for their wintering areas to the south. They are found where there is dense, brushy growth; along the roadbanks, in forest clearings, along stream borders, and in old fields. Males sing throughout the day during the breeding season from an exposed perch. Weedtops, trees, and utility wires are favorite locations for this activity. It is one of the most common species seen sitting on utility wires through mid-summer, especially in the agricultural areas surrounding the park.

Places where you should be able to find the bird include Oconaluftee and Sugarlands visitor centers, Cades Cove, Cherokee Orchard, and the lower reaches of the Newfound Gap Road. But don't be surprised to find an occasional Indigo Bunting at the higher elevations. The current loss of the spruce and fir trees has created brushy open tangles that this bunting prefers for its nesting.

Pipilo erythrophthalmus
8½ in (22 cm)

EASTERN TOWHEE

G. Ron Austing

This towhee is a permanent resident in the park. It is common up to about 3,500 feet and fairly common above this altitude during the warmer months. In the high areas of the park the bird can be found in brushy clearings in the spruce-fir forests, in tangles along watercourses, and on the heath balds and the edges of grassy balds. In the lower reaches of the park, look for it in places with dense brushy cover, including old fields, roadside edges, field borders, forest openings, and plantings around buildings. Towhees spend most of their time on the ground where they search for food by turning over leaves to get at the insects beneath. When the leaves are dry, this is a noisy activity and can aid you in locating the birds. The male sings from an exposed perch that may be in the treetops. Its *drink your teeeeeee* song is distinctive.

This towhee was formerly called "rufous-sided" in reference to the chestnut orange sides plainly visible on both adult males and females. It has also been called the "ground robin." The species name, *erythrophthalmus*, comes from the Greek for "red-eyed," and if you are close enough you will see that this is descriptive as well.

CHIPPING SPARROW

Spizella passerina
5½ in (14 cm)

J. Wedge/Vireo

6	
5	
4	
3	
2	
1	

S W M

These small sparrows are common summer residents in the lower elevations, chiefly below 3,000 feet. Occasionally you may find one in the high regions of the park; they have been seen in the Clingmans Dome parking area and at Newfound Gap. The Chipping Sparrow usually arrives here in the first two weeks of March and may be found into late November. In a few years the species has remained during the winter. It prefers clearings or park-like stands of trees where the grasses are short or sparse. Lawns meet its requirements and it is a common "yard-bird" in the communities and agricultural areas surrounding the park. Look for it around Sugarlands Visitor Center, park headquarters, Oconaluftee, and at Cades Cove near the Cable Mill and in the campground. In the park this is the only sparrow with a bright chestnut-brown cap.

For many bird enthusiasts, trying to identify bird species by their songs seems difficult, if not impossible. But everyone can identify a few species such as Blue Jays, crows, chickadees, and others. The Chipping Sparrow uses one of the easiest songs to learn. The song is a series of chip notes given in a trill, all on one pitch; *chip, chip, chip, chip, chip, chip*, etc., in machine gun fashion. Listen in suitable habitat almost any day between late March and early June and you will almost certainly hear a Chipping Sparrow sing.

Spizella pusilla
5¾ in (15 cm)

FIELD SPARROW

Fred J. Alsop III

Field Sparrows are common permanent residents in the lowlands up to the middle elevations. They have been seen in some of the high regions of the park and a few breed on the grassy bald areas such as Gregory Bald, Parson Bald, Russell Field, and Spence Field. Open areas are the bird's primary habitat, places with brushy fields, abandoned farmlands, or pasture lands with scrubby borders. Good locations in which to find the species in the park include Cades Cove, Oconaluftee, and Cataloochee. Field Sparrows may begin their singing as early as January. On summer nights when the moon is full you may hear its sweet, melancholy notes drifting across the darkened fields.

To many beginning birders the identification of sparrows is somewhat confusing and all are sometimes lumped together as "SBBs" (small, brown birds). One of the tricks to sparrow identification is to split them into two general categories: those with spots and streaks on their underparts and those without. This initial separation, followed by checks for streaked crowns, wing bars, and the presence of eye rings or eye lines can effectively put each species in its proper place. The Field Sparrow is a "plain breasted" species with two white wing bars, a white eye ring, and pink bill.

SONG SPARROW

Melospiza melodia
6¼ in (16 cm)

Fred J. Alsop III

The Song Sparrow is a common permanent resident in the lower elevations of the park. During the breeding season, however, it may be found at any altitude where there are openings in the forest or clearings with brushy undergrowth. Like Chestnut-sided Warblers and Gray Catbirds, it may be found in disturbed areas on the higher slopes. In the lowlands, look for it in wet brushy places, in thickets, along watercourses where there are tangles, and in the shrubs planted around buildings. Some good locations include Cades Cove, Sugarlands Visitor Center, Oconaluftee Visitor Center, and Elkmont.

The heavily-streaked underparts with the large dark spot in the center of the chest are identifying field marks. Songs may be heard as early as February and continue well into the late summer. The song is three or four clear introductory notes followed by a buzzy trill. The Song Sparrow spends much of its time on the ground. They are inquisitive birds and are quick to investigate any disturbance in their home area. Making squeaking noises on the back of your hand, or *pishing* sounds with your lips will often bring the bird into view. This should be the easiest sparrow for you to locate in the park at any season.

WHITE-THROATED SPARROW

Zonotrichia albicollis
6¾ in (17 cm)

G. Ron Austing

This sparrow is a common to abundant winter resident found primarily below 2,500 feet. White-throats arrive in late September or early October and may remain well past the first week of May. Their *poor-sam-peabody-peabody-peabody* song can be heard at any month they are present, but it is much more common after mid-February. Tangles and brushy places at the forest edge are good places to find this large sparrow with the striped crown and yellow lores. It is an inquisitive bird that will usually respond to squeaking noises produced by "kissing" the back of your hand. Often its *chips* of protest will also bring others of the flock into view. Much of their time is spent on the ground or close to it in thickets and weed tangles.

Two color phases of the White-throated Sparrow are now recognized. Some adult birds have head stripes of black and white, but others are a tan-striped phase with black and tan stripes in the crown. In proper season this is an easy bird to locate in almost any brushy tangle. Look for it near Sugarlands Visitor Center by the bus parking areas, and between the visitor center and the park headquarters building.

DARK-EYED JUNCO

Junco hyemalis
6¼ in (16 cm)

Fred J. Alsop III

The junco is a permanent resident in the park. It is common below 3,000 feet from October through mid-April, when nonbreeding birds move down to these more sheltered areas and are joined there by others from more northern regions. It is a fairly common breeding species above 2,600 feet from late April into October, and is most abundant in the highest elevations. It is the most common bird you will see in the spruce-fir forests in the breeding season. A census I conducted in June, 1967 on Mt. Guyot indicated a breeding density of 76 territorial males per 100 acres. Juncos are called "snowbirds" by locals because their appearance in the low elevations in the fall is a signal that winter is coming. Their scientific name *hyemalis* is New Latin for "wintry."

Take a good look at the juncos you see in the park because the resident population is a subspecies formerly called the Carolina Slate-colored Junco (*J.h. carolinensis*) that is readily separated in the field from wintering juncos of the more northern races. Note this race's larger size, its grayer color (devoid of a brown cast in the adult males), and its pale gray to horn-colored bill (flesh-colored in northern races). The "Carolina Junco" populations undergo a vertical migration in fall and spring, wintering primarily in the lower elevations instead of making the longer horizontal migrations which the northern birds make.

Agelaius phoeniceus
8¾ in (22 cm)

RED-WINGED BLACKBIRD

6	
5	
4	
3	
2	
1	
S W M	

G. Ron Austing

Like the Eastern Meadowlark and other species that require disturbed areas or marshes, the red-wing is more common in the agricultural areas outside the park. The Red-winged Blackbird is a fairly common spring and fall transient. It appears in sizable flocks in the lower elevations where it is a common breeder in proper habitat. The birds are rare here in winter.

Cades Cove is the best place to find the species. Good places to look are the brushy borders of Abrams Creek, the small branches that drain into Abrams, and fields where the grass is tall. However, in recent years red-wings have become so common as breeding birds in the cove that almost any hayfield where the grass is high will have a nesting population in summer. These gregarious birds, particularly the territorial males, are usually very conspicuous on their singing perches and in their chase flights over the fields. Any crow that crosses a colony's territory during nesting season gets a noisy and aggressive escort of diving and pecking red-wings until he is well clear of the area.

EASTERN MEADOWLARK

Sturnella magna
9½ in (24 cm)

G. Ron Austing

This member of the blackbird subfamily is a common permanent resident in Cades Cove and in the agricultural areas surrounding the park. There are few cleared areas in the park that are large enough to attract meadowlarks as nesting birds. As transients during migration seasons, these birds have been observed in spring, fall, and winter along the roadsides in high elevations (Indian Gap and Newfound Gap) and on some of the high grassy balds such as Russell Field and Spence Field.

Cades Cove, however, is the best place to see meadowlarks in the park. You will see their white outer tail feathers as they fly away or their black V breastband as they perch on the fences and walk across the ground jerking their tail open with a nervous flick. The grassy fields around the Oconaluftee Visitor Center also have resident meadowlarks.

Eastern Meadowlarks feed on grass and weed seeds in the winter and on large insects such as grasshoppers in the summer and fall. Meadowlarks are rather solitary birds during the breeding season, but they occur in flocks at other times of the year that may number from a dozen or so to groups of over a hundred.

Quiscalus quiscula
10–12½ in (25–31.7 cm)

COMMON GRACKLE

J. Schumacher/Vireo

These rather large blackbirds are permanent residents that are fairly common in the lower elevations during summer. They are rare to uncommon in winter. Cades Cove is one of the best places to see them, but they are sometimes found around the Sugarlands Visitor Center. Grackles can be seen in flocks with other species of blackbirds and starlings in the nonbreeding season, especially outside the park. Much of their time is spent on the ground.

The large keeled tail is one of the best field marks and is noticeable even at considerable distances. The males are larger than the females and adults of both sexes have bright yellow eyes. Grackles often nest in small, loose colonies in conifers such as white pine and red cedar. Common Grackles feed heavily on large insects during the summer and seem especially fond of the large white grubs that are the larval stage of ground burrowing beetles. During the colder months of the year they supplement their insect diet with seeds, grains, fruits, and nuts. The song is squeaky and metallic and has been likened to the sound of a barnyard gate swinging on rusty hinges.

BROWN-HEADED COWBIRD

Molothrus ater
7½ in (19 cm)

G. Ron Austing

6	
5	
4	
3	
2	
1	///////

S W M

This is a permanent resident that is scarce in winter, fairly common in summer and fall, and common in late March, April, and early May. It occurs in the park chiefly below 2,000 feet. For most of the year cowbirds travel in flocks, but in the breeding season pairs, or small groups with males outnumbering the females, are usually seen. Cades Cove is perhaps the best place to look, as cowbirds are often found in the fields near the grazing cattle.

The scientific name can be translated to "black parasite," and the cowbird is our only Eastern songbird that is a brood parasite. The female selects the active nest of another species of songbird and lays her eggs there, often removing an egg of the host for each one she lays. Open cup nests are frequently chosen and favorite host species include the Red-eyed Vireo, Yellow Warbler, and Song Sparrow. Fledgling cowbirds seem to be perpetually famished and my attention has often been drawn to the sight of a scurrying vireo or Song Sparrow feverishly trying to collect and transport insect after insect to the gaping mouth of its constantly calling "baby" cowbird. The foster child is often considerably larger than the attendant "parent."

Icterus spurius

7¼ in (18 cm)

ORCHARD ORIOLE

B. Schorre/Vireo

This small oriole is an uncommon transient and an uncommon summer resident in the park, generally found in the lower elevations below 2,000 feet. It arrives in the last week of April and departs by the first week of September. It is a common summer resident in the agricultural areas just outside the park, especially to the north and west. Some of the best places to look are open areas with scattered trees along roads, streams, or around homesteads.

Within the park try Cades Cove, Oconaluftee Visitor Center, Cherokee Orchard, and Sugarlands Visitor Center. In recent years I have often found a territorial male in the line of trees bordering the south side of the Cades Cove sewage lagoon. The nest is an open pouch not nearly as deep as the six-inch deep bag woven by the Northern (Baltimore) Oriole. It is not placed as far out toward the tips of the branches either, but suspended in a fork between them. The heavily-forested areas that cover most of the park provide little habitat for this oriole.

Male Orchard Orioles are burnt orange above and below with black hoods, wings, and tails. They lack the bright orange coloration of the larger Northern Oriole. Females are dull olive above and greenish-yellow below, with two white wing bars.

PURPLE FINCH

Carpodacus purpureus
6 in (15 cm)

Fred J. Alsop III

6	
5	
4	
3	
2	
1	
S W M	

The Purple Finch is a winter resident whose status varies from year to year in the park. It is common in some years and virtually absent in others. During its stay here it can be found at any elevation in flocks ranging in size from just a few individuals to 20 or more. The birds often feed in the treetops on seeds, but some may forage on the ground. "Purple" is a misnomer, for the male is really not purple at all, but shows raspberry or wine-colored areas on head, breast, and rump. The grounds around the Sugarlands Visitor Center often have these northern finches when they are present in the Smokies. Stands of tulip trees, *Liriodendron tulipifera*, are especially attractive to these finches in the fall. Watch for bits of seeds falling from the treetops as a clue to their presence.

Until recently the only small finch in the park that looked like a Purple Finch was a Purple Finch. But, beginning in the mid-1980s, the first observations of the similar House Finch (*C. mexicanus*) were made. House Finches are a non-native species in the park and should be reported to park ranger stations or visitor centers. Park biologists are monitoring their numbers.

Carduelis pinus
5 in (13 cm)

PINE SISKIN

Fred J. Alsop III

Siskins have been observed in the park in every month of the year, but their numbers are very erratic. For the most part it is considered an irregular winter resident with the majority of birds arriving in the second week of October and departing by mid-May. In some winters this little finch is abundant with flocks numbering in the hundreds or thousands, and in others only one or two birds may be seen all season. In the summer and early fall siskins are found chiefly above 4,800 feet. Then you may find them feeding on the leaves, petals, and seeds of dandelions along the roadsides. At other months they occur at all elevations. They are frequently in mixed flocks with goldfinches, which they resemble. One should look at each goldfinch flock for the siskin that might be there.

Siskins are usually associated with coniferous forests and much of their diet in the park is made up of seeds extracted from Eastern hemlock, red spruce, and various pine species.

The siskin is one of those species in the park that biologists would like to know more about. Sometimes it is present during the nesting season, but there is no proof that nesting has taken place. Any observations of nesting should be reported at park visitor centers.

AMERICAN GOLDFINCH

Carduelis tristis
5 in (13 cm)

Fred J. Alsop III

These "wild canaries" are fairly common permanent residents that occur at all elevations, but they are much more common below 4,500 feet. They are gregarious birds and are usually found in small flocks during most of the year. In early spring the flocks are sometimes larger, numbering a hundred or more individuals. Dandelions are an especially attractive food in April and May and you will find them feeding on thistle seeds in August and September.

Goldfinches are the latest birds in getting their nesting activities underway in the park. They begin nest construction in late July, August, and into September after almost all other songbirds have raised their broods and begun their post-breeding molts. The nest is usually placed in a weedy patch, particularly one with thistle nearby, or in small trees. Thistle is important as a downy lining for the nest (the silky tassels attached to the seeds are used) and the seeds are fed to the nestlings. The Sugarlands Visitor Center area, Cades Cove, and Oconaluftee are but a few places you may find goldfinches. Watch the roadsides all the way up into the spruce-fir zone when the dandelions are flowering.

Goldfinches fly with a roller coaster, undulating flight. Their breeding season flight song is *per-chic-o-ree*.

8 in (20 cm)

Fred J. Alsop III

This handsome finch of the northern forests was first observed in the park in 1951. It is an erratic winter visitor, being absent sometimes for several winters. When present, usually from early November through mid-May, it may be found at all elevations of the park, but is most frequently seen in the trees around park headquarters and at bird feeders in Gatlinburg. Evening Grosbeaks are often encountered in flocks and you may first be alerted to them by their House Sparrow-like calls.

The name "grosbeak" refers to their very large, cone-shaped beaks which are specialized for cracking the tough coats surrounding seeds. The jaw-breaking genus name, *Coccothraustes*, is also a reference to this bird's seed-cracking abilities; it is from the Greek for "kernel-breaker."

Wild fruits and seeds that are eaten by Evening Grosbeaks in the park and surrounding areas include flowering dogwood, sumac, tulip tree, yellow birch, red maple, American mountain-ash, and red spruce. They are attracted to salt and salt-impregnated earth and are sometimes seen on the edges of roadways after snowplows have passed.

THE BIRDER'S DOZEN

Most birders who travel to the park want to see as many species as possible during their visit, but there often seems to be one particular bird, or perhaps several, that are sought after with special effort. The following 12 species are the ones I have been asked about most in over two decades of birding in the Smokies. So, here are my dozen-most-wanted-species and the places where I have been the most successful in finding them.

NORTHERN SAW-WHET OWL · · · · · · · · · · · · · · · · · ·

This, the smallest owl in eastern North America, is an uncommon permanent resident in the park. The best time to locate it is spring and early summer when the birds are singing. Though songs have been recorded from mid-March well into June, the peak of singing activity is from the first week of April through the third week of May. At this time of year the birds are in the higher elevations, principally in the Canadian zone spruce-fir forests above 5,000 feet.

Weather conditions seem to be a major factor influencing singing, with most vocalizations coming on clear nights with little or no wind. Rain, fog, low clouds, and other inclement conditions make the chances of hearing this owl almost zero. Moonlit nights seem to be more productive than dark ones, but any clear, windless night in the proper season can be good. Drive up to Newfound Gap parking area, timing your arrival for about one hour after sunset. Leave the car and walk the boundaries of the parking area, listening for the monotonous, single whistled notes of the Saw-whet, *whot-whot-whot-whot*, about two per second for up to several minutes.

The sound carries well in these high silent forests and may be heard for more than a mile. Cupping your hands behind your ears will improve your hearing. The owls can be heard at elevations slightly lower than Newfound Gap on the Tennessee side of the park. Leave Newfound Gap and continue south (left turn out of the parking lot) to the Clingmans Dome Road turnoff. Follow the road to Clingmans Dome parking area (7.5 miles), stopping and listening at every pulloff until you either find the owl or decide tonight is just not your night.

I have found from one to 11 birds singing in a single night between Newfound Gap and Clingmans Dome, although there have been many nights when I heard none, even though all the conditions seemed right. The birds may be heard at any hour of the night and some individuals sing all night long. There have been occasional reports of Saw-whets singing during the day. In recent years the "hottest" spots have been Newfound Gap parking area, Indian Gap, and the stretch of the Clingmans Dome road beginning at the Spruce-fir Nature Trail and extending north (downhill) for 1.5 miles. I have rarely had this bird respond to a tape recorder or to my whistled imitation of its voice. I have even played a tape of a Saw-whet's song directly beneath a singing bird. The only difference in the real owl's behavior was that it sang more rapidly. However, tapes made of birds in the Smokies sometimes produce better results.

SWAINSON'S WARBLER ·

Since this warbler was first recorded in the park in 1950, it has been searched for frequently by birders. Look for it in rhododendron thickets, especially those associated with wet ravines or small streams, below an elevation of 2,300 feet. You will hear this bird much more often than you will see it. Its presence is announced by a loud ringing voice from the tangles. The song has a ventriloquistic effect. A bird singing on the ground may sound like it's several feet above the forest floor. The warbler is not overly shy, and a quiet approach will often be rewarded by good views of the singer.

Territorial birds can be heard singing from the last week of April well into June. Learn the song, *whee, whee, whee, whip-poor-will*, before you search and be aware that the song of the much more common Louisiana Waterthrush is similar. There are probably many places to find the bird in the park, but the following locations have been good for several years.

Gatlinburg entrance to the park. Park your car in the pull-off just north of the park entrance sign (the large wooden sign where visitors pose for photos), lock it, and walk south along the road shoulder until you reach the area marked "turn around" and "no parking." Standing in this paved area it is often possible to hear a Swainson's Warbler singing just a few yards inside the woodland border as you face away from the highway. Follow the unmarked pathway into the woods to where it bisects a wider walking path within approximately 50 feet. Turn left onto the trail. The thickets of rhododendron and small hemlock trees just between this walkway and the highway have had a territorial male for many years. Failing to locate the warbler here, walk the paved path on southward and check in the rhododendron thickets that border it for the next 1,000 yards or so. Returning to your car, continue on southward into the park and stop at the "Riding Stable" on the left (less than one mile). A Swainson's Warbler has been found in the rhododendron thickets adjacent to the parking areas and along the stream near the stable and corrals.

Sugarlands Visitor Center. A Swainson's Warbler can usually be heard singing just east of the visitor center. The bird frequents the rhododendron just across the Newfound Gap Road near the junction with Little River Road. The first 200 yards of the Sugarlands Nature Trail often produce a territorial Swainson's Warbler.

White Oak Sinks/Bote Mountain trails. Look for the unpaved roads behind locked gates approximately 100 yards apart on the Laurel Creek Road about four miles west of the Townsend "Y." Park at the Schoolhouse Gap trailhead on the right (north) and walk the first 1,000 yards listening for the Swainson's Warbler in the rhododendron thickets. Upon returning to the paved road, walk downhill (east) to the Bote Mountain trailhead and check the first 1,000 yards or so of this area. The birds sing almost all day and can be heard at midday if you don't want to be in the field by dawn.

RED CROSSBILL · · · · · · · · · · · · · · · · ·

This is a most erratic species in the park by places of occurrence and in numbers of individuals. It is present during every month of the year and is most often reported from June through September in the higher elevations. Birds sometimes frequent the shelters along the Appalachian Trail, especially those between Silers Bald and Tricorner Knob, where they are reportedly seeking salt. I can tell you of no one place where you can have even a 50–50 chance of seeing Red Crossbills on a given day, however, if you know the *jip-jip-jip* notes given in flight, you have a reasonable chance of detecting the birds as they fly over the mountainsides. I have had good luck in seeing crossbills at Indian Gap and Collins Gap on the road to Clingmans Dome as well as the parking area near Clingmans Dome. I have also seen them picking up small gravels almost at visitors' feet along the walkways at Newfound Gap parking area. Watch for them on the ground along the road edges and in conifers with large cones.

WILD TURKEY · · · · · · · · · · · · · · · · · ·

This is an uncommon permanent resident that occurs at almost all elevations in the park, but probably your best chance of seeing one, or several, is by birding Cades Cove. As you drive the loop road, watch the fields and scan the tree lines with binoculars. The birds often feed in the cover of the woods where they are difficult to detect. The best spot in the cove in recent years has been the fields and woodlots around the Methodist Church at marker #5. Stop at the church cemetery and scan the fields below. Cross the road and walk east (against the traffic flow) for 100 yards, checking the fields on both sides of the road.

Turn at marker #6 onto Hyatt Lane, a two-way road, and drive as far as the creek. Search the fields, especially those on your left (east), for turkey as you drive. The trees along the creek often harbor songbirds and the cherry trees that border the lane attract many birds in summer. Do your birding in Cades Cove as early as possible, before visitor traffic begins to build up and people start to walk in the fields. I have found weekdays and the off-season (November to April) to be more productive because of fewer visitors.

COMMON RAVEN · · · · · · · · · · · · · · · · · ·

This big ebony bird is a fairly common permanent resident most often seen in the higher elevations of the park. During winter it is occasionally seen in the lowlands. The birder's best bet is to frequent the upper reaches of the Newfound Gap Road and the entire Clingmans Dome Road. Scan the skies; ravens like to soar, and listen for their *cronk, cronk, cronk* calls. I have often seen this bird at Newfound Gap, Indian Gap, and Clingmans Dome parking areas. Be aware that American Crows frequent all elevations, even the high spruce-fir forests, and are the large black birds most often seen along the roadsides.

For many years ravens have nested on Peregrine Peak in a cliff site that can be seen from the Alum Cave Trail just before you reach Alum Cave. Scan the cliff face for a large stick nest across the valley opposite the trail. In April and May there should be adult birds about if the nest is active.

PILEATED WOODPECKER · · · · · · · · · · · · · · ·

Because of the huge tracts of forest covered by Pileated Woodpeckers, they are difficult to "pin" to any one location. However, these fairly common, permanent residents are large and often noisy. When drumming on a dead limb, their raps carry a considerable distance. The tree sounds like it is being struck with a wooden mallet, a sound much louder than that produced by other local woodpeckers. They call rather infrequently, but their loud cries catch your ears and ring of a "jungle" sound of Hollywood origins. You may see these birds as they fly from ridge top to ridge top, crossing high above the valleys.

Pileated Woodpeckers occur at all elevations in the park, but are more common in the hardwoods, especially in the lowlands. The birds often feed on stumps and fallen logs that harbor boring insects. One good place to look in Cades Cove is near the end of the loop road where it crosses the horse trail. Check the mixed pine and hardwood stands along the horse trail leading to the Cades Cove sewage lagoon. Also scan the area from the horse trail intersection back to the campground store.

KENTUCKY WARBLER · · · · · · · · · · · · · · · ·

You will hear many more Kentucky Warblers than you will see. It is a common summer resident from the third week of April through the last of September. Look for it in the hardwood forests below 3,500 feet. It is a very vocal species but is often difficult to see because it feeds and nests on the forest floor and forages in the scrubby growth near the ground. Kentucky Warblers respond well to squeaking sounds made by "kissing" the back of your hand or to imitations of a screech-owl's call. They will often come quite close to the source of the sounds while constantly giving their own alarm notes.

Almost any of the deep-shaded woodlands in the lower elevations have this warbler in the nesting season. Especially good places are those with ground cover to conceal the nest and the sides of ravines. Three good places to start your search within a few minutes of downtown Gatlinburg are the Sugarlands Visitor Center, Roaring Fork Motor Nature Trail, and Maloney Point. At Sugarlands, walk the self-guiding nature trail (one mile) and try the woodlands surrounding the trailer dumping station across the road from the visitor center parking areas.

Roaring Fork Motor Nature Trail starts on Airport Road 2½ miles from midtown Gatlinburg. Stop at the wooded turnouts. Those near Cherokee Orchard, with its abandoned apple trees and nesting American Redstarts, have always produced Kentucky Warblers. Maloney Point is on Little River Road approximately 3½ miles west of Sugarlands Visitor Center. There are three pullouts only a few hundred yards apart, and I frequently find the warbler downhill from the second and third parking areas.

WORM-EATING WARBLER · · · · · · · · · · · · · ·

This species is a fairly common summer resident. It's found in the lowlands up to about 3,000 feet from the third week of April well into September. Like the Kentucky Warbler, it is a ground nesting species and you should look for it in the same habitats and locations as the Kentucky Warbler. Its dry, buzzy trill will usually be your first indication of the bird's presence, and like the Kentucky Warbler, its songs are given frequently throughout the day from late April into early July. Other species to be found in the same woodlands include the Black-and-white Warbler, Hooded Warbler, Kentucky Warbler, Carolina Wren, Red-eyed Vireo, Wood Thrush, and the Ovenbird.

As with the Kentucky Warbler, a little silent stalking in the woodlands in proper season should produce this attractive warbler. Two good spots, easily reached, are the scenic overlooks on the Gatlinburg Bypass. Stop at both and you should locate this warbler as well as the Kentucky Warbler. Maloney Point (see Kentucky Warbler) has also been productive for this species in recent years. Try the little ravine across the road (south side) between the second and third pullouts.

OLIVE-SIDED FLYCATCHER · · · · · · · · · · · · · · · · · ·

This large flycatcher is an uncommon summer resident from late April through mid-September in the higher elevations. It is usually first sighted high on some conspicuous treetop from which it hawks flying insects. Or you may first hear its carrying song of *what, three cheers,* or *quick, three beers.* The two most frequent places where the bird has been reported are the Newfound Gap parking area and its surrounding boreal forest and the Alum Cave Trail between Arch Rock and Alum Cave. Arch Rock is 1¼ miles from the trailhead on the Newfound Gap Road and the cave is another 1¼ miles further.

BLACK-CAPPED CHICKADEE · · · · · · · · · · · · · · · · · ·

This fairly common permanent resident is the larger of the two chickadee species that occur in the park. Both it and the Carolina Chickadee are very similar in appearance and generally the easiest way to separate these species is by voice and elevation—neither are infallible, however. The song of the Black-capped Chickadee is *fee-bee-ee* or *fee-bee* while that of the Carolina is a thinner four noted *fee-bee, fee-bu*. During the breeding season, the Black-capped is the chickadee of the higher elevations down to around 4,000 feet while the Carolina Chickadee is found mostly below this elevation.

As a rule-of-thumb, any chickadee you find in the spruce-fir forest will be a Black-capped. Any short walk into the forest from Clingmans Dome to just below Newfound Gap should produce this species. In the nonbreeding season it often forages in mixed flocks with Brown Creepers, Golden-crowned Kinglets, and Red-breasted Nuthatches. During the winter months some individuals move downward into the middle elevations occupied by Carolina Chickadees. The bird is usually quite bold and will often allow the birder a reasonably close approach. Close observation will reveal more white on the coverts and secondaries of the folded wing than on a Carolina Chickadee.

CANADA WARBLER ·

This bright yellow and gray warbler is a common summer resident above 3,400 feet from the third week of April well into September. It prefers dark tangles of rhododendron, especially along stream courses, and it is from these you will hear its song from its arrival in April through most of July. The bird responds well to squeaking noises and can often be lured in close for a better view by the birder.

Try any rhododendron thicket in the higher elevations and you should have little trouble in adding the Canada Warbler to your list. Two of my favorite places are just up the Alum Cave Trail and the first pulloff on the Newfound Gap Road on the North Carolina side below Newfound Gap. The Alum Cave Trail parallels a rushing mountain stream and is bordered on both sides by great stands of rhododendron where Canada Warblers abound. The only disadvantage to the trail is that the stream makes listening for bird songs difficult.

The parking area on the North Carolina side below Newfound

Gap is backed by a mountainside of rhododendron. One can usually find Canada Warblers, Black-throated Blue Warblers, Black-throated Green Warblers, Solitary Vireos, and several other species there without leaving the paved parking area. The blackberry tangles on both sides of the highway and a few hundred yards on down the road from this parking area have nesting Chestnut-sided Warblers during the same season that you will be searching for the Canadas. Blackburnian Warblers also nest in the surrounding forests, especially the spruce-fir, and with a little luck you can check off all five of the high-altitude warbler species that occur in the park.

BLACK-THROATED BLUE WARBLER · · · · · · · · · · · ·

This attractive warbler is a common summer resident above 2,800 feet in the park. It can be found from mid-April into October and there are records into November. The song is delivered from first arrival into September and is given throughout the day. The bird is often associated with breaks and disturbed areas in the forest and frequents rhododendron tangles. If you are driving up the Newfound Gap Road from Gatlinburg, the first place you can count on locating this species is in the Chimneys Picnic Area five miles south of Sugarlands Visitor Center. Walk the paved road paying particular attention to the rhododendron thickets uphill from the picnic grounds, as the birds nest here. Walking the Cove Hardwood Nature Trail (¾ mile loop) will almost always produce several Black-throated Blues, as well as Solitary Vireos, and the Appalachian race of the Dark-eyed Junco.

Back on the Newfound Gap Road, the first pull-offs that give you a view of the Chimney Tops are also good places to stop and look for the Black-throated Blue Warbler, Scarlet Tanager, Rose-breasted Grosbeak, and many other species. Around the Chimney Tops trailhead is another good place to look for the warbler, as is almost any spot from there on up to Clingmans Dome. The locations listed for the Canada Warbler are also places where you should be successful in finding Black-throated Blue Warblers.

BIRD FINDING IN THE PARK

For those whose time in Great Smoky Mountains National Park is limited, but who would like to see as many species of birds as possible, I have outlined several of my favorite birding trips. Each trip involves spending several hours to a day in the field and is based on getting to the locations by automobile and then taking short walks. Of course not every species in an area will be listed, but characteristic birds as well as any local "rarities" will be noted. So don't just read the information and put it aside, get out with those binoculars and field guides and try each one out.

Birding from the Lowlands to "Canada." Roundtrip driving distance from Gatlinburg: 49 miles. Walking distance: 3-5 miles. In the high elevations of these mountains, many birds common in more northern forests reach the southern limits of their breeding range. Spring migration and the summer nesting season are the best times to see the most birds, but many winters bring northern finches in numbers not found elsewhere in the surrounding states.

From Gatlinburg, take Airport Road south to Cherokee Orchard Road. Follow the road past the Noah "Bud" Ogle farm and through regrown forests. En route, when you reach the parking areas for the Rainbow Falls Trail, park your auto and walk along the road in the direction of the traffic flow to the area where aged apple trees grow. In spring and summer this is a particularly good place to see nesting American Redstarts and along the short walk you should have the Indigo Bunting, Eastern Towhee, Kentucky Warbler, and Ovenbird. In the woodlands, look for the Red-eyed Vireo, Carolina Chickadee, Tufted Titmouse, Carolina Wren, Scarlet Tanager. and Blue-gray Gnatcatcher. Watch in the more open areas for Ruby-throated Hummingbirds. Golden-winged Warblers (uncommon) have been found in the weedy openings as well. Barred Owls can sometimes be heard calling here during the day. A nighttime visit to these parking areas, especially in spring and summer, is almost sure to produce this owl, particularly if you imitate its call or play a recording of it.

In summer, watch overhead for Chimney Swifts and Broad-winged Hawks. The singing Wood Thrush of summer will give way to the Hermit Thrush in the winter months. As you return to your car, listen for the explosive sneeze *peeup* of another summer resident, the Acadian Flycatcher. Back in your car, follow the signs to Gatlinburg without driving the Roaring Fork Motor Nature Trail (the latter makes a good half-day birding trip if you have the time on another outing).

In town, follow U.S. 441 south to Sugarlands Visitor Center. Here you will find excellent displays on the plant and animal life, maps of the park, field guides, and a bird checklist. In winter, search the grounds of park headquarters just a few hundred yards north of the visitor center for Purple Finch, Pine Siskin, and Evening Grosbeak. Walk the self-guiding Sugarlands Nature Trail in spring and summer for Black-and-white, Kentucky, and Hooded warblers, Ovenbird, Wood Thrush, Louisiana Waterthrush, Northern Parula, Red-eyed Vireo, Yellow-throated Vireo, and many other songbirds. Barn Swallows and Eastern Phoebes usually nest under the eaves of the visitor center.

Go back on the Newfound Gap Road and turn right (south) towards Cherokee, N.C. Stop at Campbell Overlook, approximately two miles from the visitor center on the left, for an open view of Mt. Le Conte. This can be a very good place to observe spring migrants. Proceed south to Chimneys Picnic Area five miles from the visitor center. A walk through these grounds, or the Cove Hardwoods Nature Trail (¾ mile loop), in the nesting season should produce American Redstarts, Wood Thrushes, Black-throated Blue Warblers, Blue-headed Vireos, and many others. Go on to Chimney Tops parking area and walk down to the heath bald on the right. Rose-breasted Grosbeaks and Scarlet Tanagers nest in the hardwood forest and Chestnut-sided Warblers nest in the rhododendron. Continue on south to Alum Cave Trail parking area on the left about 8½ miles from the visitor center. The Alum Cave Trail is moderately steep but well worth the effort. It is 2½ miles by trail to Alum Cave through northern hardwood forests inhabited in summer by Red-eyed and Blue-headed vireos, Wood

Thrush, Veery, Carolina and Winter wrens, Olive-sided and Great Crested flycatchers, Black-throated Blue, Blackburnian, and Canada warblers. Before you reach the bluffs you will climb through heath balds where Chestnut-sided Warblers abound. The ridge opposite the bluff is a nesting site for the Peregrine Falcon, a species extirpated from the park from 1944 to 1984. Six young Peregrines were "hacked" or released in the park in 1984 and again in 1985 in an effort to reestablish the species here. A pair of Peregrines has successfully nested in the park annually beginning in the mid-to-late 1990s. The peak is also sometimes used as a nesting place by the Common Raven. Another 2.9 miles up the trail will bring you to the top of Mt. Le Conte where there is a lodge (reservations required).

Back at your car, continue south to Newfound Gap. You have now entered the Canadian life zone characterized by the dominant forest of spruce and fir. Temperatures here are much lower than at Sugarlands, about 15-20 degrees F., and rain showers are more frequent, so be prepared. You will notice many dead conifers, mostly Fraser fir, that have succumbed to attack by balsam woolly adelgids and perhaps acid rain. Cedar Waxwings, Red Crossbills, and Pine Siskins are often seen near the parking area at any season.

Birds seen from here upward to Clingmans Dome parking area, via stops at Indian Gap, Collins Gap, and a walk along the Spruce-fir Nature Trail (all along your route) will include these summer residents: the five high-altitude warblers; Canada, Blackburnian, Black-throated Blue, Black-throated Green, and Chestnut-sided; plus Veerys and Blue-headed Vireos. Permanent residents are Common Raven, Golden-crowned Kinglet, Red Crossbill, Red-breasted Nuthatch, Brown Creeper, Black-capped Chickadee, and the most abundant resident of the spruce-fir, the Dark-eyed Junco. Ruffed Grouse occur at all elevations in the park and most are seen early in the morning and late in the evenings along the road shoulders. They have been recorded drumming during every month of the year, with the most records in October.

From the Clingmans Dome parking area a ½ mile paved trail takes you to an observation tower atop the highest mountain in

the park, Clingmans Dome, elevation 6,643 feet. If you stop at all
the pull-offs between Clingmans Dome and Morton Overlook (just
below Newfound Gap on the Tennessee side) in the spring and
summer after dark you may hear the Barred Owl and the less
common Northern Saw-whet Owl.

The best conditions for the Saw-whet are nights of little wind
and some moonlight between the end of March and the middle of
June; Most singing is recorded during this season, but the owls
have been seen at other times of the year. Whistled imitations,
tape recordings, and "squeaking" on your hand have all been tried
with varying success to lure these dwarfs of the boreal forest out to
be counted. An evening's foray has produced Saw-whets in
numbers from zero to 11 along this route.

The Cades Cove Loop Road. Roundtrip driving distance from
Gatlinburg: 65 miles, from Cherokee: 123 miles. Walking distance:
about three miles. Many birds common to the lowlands of East
Tennessee can be observed from the comfort of your automobile
and along the numerous trails that follow the gentle contours of
this mountain valley. This pioneer setting with split rail fences, log
cabins, and frame churches surrounded by a backdrop of hazy
mountains provides a unique atmosphere to browsing deer,
scurrying groundhogs, and flocks of Wild Turkey.

Begin the trip at the Tremont "Y" at the junction of the Laurel
Creek and Little River Roads, ¼ mile south of the Townsend
entrance to the park. Park at the pulloffs around the stone bridge
and spend a few minutes birding here. In summer, Northern
Rough-winged Swallows are nesting in the drainage pipes below
the bridge and Louisiana Waterthrushes can be seen and heard
along the streams. Birds that nest in the surrounding woodlands
include Black-throated Green, Yellow-throated, Kentucky, and
Northern Parula warblers as well as American Redstarts. Scarlet
Tanagers sing from the pines on the nearby ridges.

As you drive southwest towards Cades Cove, the mountain
stream rushing beside the road is Laurel Creek. This is the summer
haunt of the Louisiana Waterthrush, whose voice is one of the

most common along the way. You will hear many Acadian Flycatchers and Black-throated Green Warblers as well. Watch for the Bote Mountain Trail approximately 3.2 miles from the "Y" on the left and the larger Schoolhouse Gap trailhead on the right a few hundred feet further.

A short walk along the Schoolhouse Gap Trail should produce Ruffed Grouse at any season as well as many small woodland species. The rhododendron thickets along the streams for the first ¼ mile in all directions from the parking area are one of the best areas for the uncommon (in the park) Swainson's Warbler from May through July. But learn the song, for you will hear many more than you will see. Other common nesting birds in this area include Red-eyed Vireos, Wood Thrushes, Northern Parula and Hooded warblers, Carolina Wrens, and the Eastern Phoebes that nest under the bridge.

Continue on to your first view of Cades Cove from the orientation shelter at the beginning of the 11-mile one-way loop. Along this drive there are numbered posts used to point out features in conjunction with the self-guiding auto tour booklet available at the shelter. I will use them to point out areas of birding interest. American Crows, Turkey Vultures, Eastern Bluebirds, and Eastern Meadowlarks are the most common avian residents seen in the valley.

At marker #2, turn left onto the gravel road (Sparks Lane). Birding along this road is good at any season, especially in the treelines along the two fords where summer produces nesting Great Crested Flycatchers, Yellow-throated Vireos, and the Northern (Baltimore) Orioles. Watch for Barn Swallows in flight, look for Wild Turkeys in the fields and listen for the Northern Bobwhite's *bobwhite* call. When you reach the paved road on the south side of the cove, turn around and retrace your path along Sparks Lane. The rather large, dark, furry mammal you have probably already seen by now is the Eastern marmot (Marmota monax) called the groundhog or woodchuck.

Return to the loop road. At marker #4, turn left to the Primitive Baptist Church. The cemetery behind the church is a good place to find waves of migrating songbirds in spring and fall. Search the fields between markers #4 and #5, especially near the wood edges, for Wild Turkey. These large birds should be looked for throughout the cove, but this is one of their favorite areas. Also check for turkey in the fields behind the Methodist Church at marker #5. At marker #6, turn left onto Hyatt Lane (gravel) and stop on top of the hill (200 yards). In the pine woods to the left (east) is a living pine with the top broken off, the tallest tree in the stand. This is the center of a vulture roost and many Turkey Vultures and a few Black Vultures are usually around. Vesper Sparrows are common in the fields in November and March and Water Pipits are seen here during most winters.

Continue to the bridge and park. The tree line along the stream attracts many birds and is about the only place in the Smokies where you might see a Red-headed Woodpecker. Eastern Bluebirds nest in the tree cavities along the creek and a Common Yellow-throat and Blue Grosbeak are usually in the weedy thickets in summer.

After birding near the bridge, retrace your route to marker #6 and turn left. Watch for Eastern Kingbirds and Eastern Bluebirds in summer along the fences. Park near the Abrams Falls turnoff and walk across the paved road (east). Slip through the gap in the fence and follow the dirt road into the fields. Bear left along the low wet areas just inside the wooded edge for approximately ½ mile until you see Abrams Creek in the open field on your left. This is the "oxbow" and a unique habitat within the park. It is the only marsh-like area in the cove. Many ducks and a few Golden Eagles rest here in winter. Golden Eagles have also been seen in the trees further upstream. King Rails have been flushed from the bullrush and tall grass in May and June and Willow Flycatchers inhabit the stream-side thickets. Eagles and rails are most uncommon in this mountainous park, but a look in the oxbow can be rewarding.

The ½ mile walk to the Elijah Oliver place (marker #10) is often very productive for woodland species. Look for Northern Parula and Yellow-throated warblers near Abrams Falls parking area in summer. Continue on the paved road past the Becky Cable cemetery and park in the lot. Walk back to the blacktop and turn right. The loop road turns abruptly right in approximately 100 yards. Walk off on the trail to the left to the "gum swamp" within sight of the road. This area, wet except during very dry periods, often attracts many birds including Northern Parula warblers, Ovenbirds, Scarlet Tanagers, Acadian Flycatchers, Great Crested Flycatchers, and Barred Owls. Wood Ducks have nested here, and Pileated Woodpeckers are often heard from this spot. In late February and early March the wood frog (*Rana sylvatica*) lays thousands of eggs in the shallow pools.

A mile or so after passing marker #17 (Shields cabin) watch for a sign warning, "Stop for horses," and a gravel road leading into the woods on the left (marked "Closed"). Park on the left and follow this road to the large fenced pond (200 yards). This is the sewage lagoon for the campground and it has attracted such unusual birds in season as Yellow-crowned Night-Heron (they have nested in the trees along the creek nearby), Green Heron, Little Blue Heron, Bonaparte's Gull, many swallows, Wood Duck and other ducks, and even one Red-necked Phalarope. The nearby woodlots are always worth birding as well. Visiting the campground and the picnic area on a summer evening should produce Whip-poor-wills, Eastern Screech-Owls, and Barred Owls. The owls can be found here at all seasons.

OWL PROWLS AND OTHER BIRDS THAT CALL IN THE NIGHT.
Some of the most exciting birding in the park occurs after the sun sinks behind the hazy mountains and the nightbirds begin to call and pursue their secretive ways. Spring and summer are the most productive (and comfortable) seasons for searching in the darkness, but there are several species that can be heard, and sometimes seen, in the dead of winter. The following species are those that you should have the best opportunity of finding, but this list does not include all the birds that may go *churp* or *hoot* in the night, just the most common ones.

◆**American Woodcock**—This upland bird is an uncommon resident in the park and the surrounding areas. It is most easily located during its singing and aerial display from mid-winter into spring. If the winter has been mild, these vocal and nonvocal sounds (the bird produces a twittering sound with its wing primaries as it spirals downward) may be heard as early as the first week of January and will continue into April.

The best places to look are overgrown fields, wet seepage areas, and woodland edges where the bird quietly spends the day and where its staple food of earthworms can be found. Locate your "spot" during the day and return just about sunset. Most of the singing and display begins about a half hour after sundown, especially on those nights when the temperature is mild and there is little wind. Songs are also given at dawn during the period of the same light intensity as the previous dusk. On moonlit nights early in the season singing may continue off-and-on all night. The *peent* note given on the ground may remind you of the call of a frog or the Common Nighthawk. Good places to listen are sites below 2,000 feet with the habitats listed above, including the Sugarlands Visitor Center, Oconaluftee, and Cades Cove.

◆**Eastern Screech-Owl**—This bird is a fairly common permanent resident found almost everywhere in woodlands below 4,000 feet. Singing has been recorded every month of the year, but most often in March and early April, when they are nesting, and from July through October, when family groups are out foraging together. The bird doesn't really screech, but commonly sings with a quavering, downward-slurring whistle often interspersed by a trill. The sound is easily imitated and either it or a recording of the call can usually lure several of these small tufted owls close enough for viewing by flashlight. Almost any time of year can be productive. The area around Sugarlands Visitor Center is good (except for the background traffic noise) and any campground in the lower elevations should be productive, as should roadside pull-offs in the lowlands.

◆**Great Horned Owl**—This is an uncommon permanent resident usually heard in the lower elevations (there are a few high altitude records) especially near the park boundaries. Singing has been recorded during every month of the year. Like the Eastern Screech-Owl, most of the singing is done just after dusk or at dawn. December and January have been the best months to hear this large tufted owl and April, May, and June have been the poorest. Great Horned Owls will sometimes respond to imitations and tapes of their calls by hooting in response and coming closer for a look at the "intruder." Within the park boundaries Cades Cove is one of the best places to try your luck.

◆**Barred Owl**—This is a fairly common permanent resident that is most often reported from above 3,500 feet, but it occurs at all elevations. Unlike most other owls here, Barred Owls can be heard calling during the day and will often respond to imitations and recordings of their calls during the day. The poorest months for singing seem to be from November to March, but this may simply reflect the fact that there are fewer birders in the park. In addition to the high elevation birds, I have often heard the familiar, *who cooks for you, who cooks for youall!* song from the campground in Cades Cove and from Rich Mountain on the north side of Cades Cove. Good places close to Gatlinburg are the Rainbow Falls parking area in Cherokee Orchard and the nearby Roaring Fork Motor Nature Trail.

◆**Northern Saw-whet Owl**—This is a fairly common permanent resident in the higher elevations, especially the spruce-fir forests. Please refer to the section headed "The Birder's Dozen" for suggestions on locating this tiny owl in the park.

◆**Chuck-will's-widow**—This species is a very uncommon summer resident and migrant in the park, but fairly common to common in late spring and summer in the coves and valleys outside the park boundaries. Tuckaleechee Cove, Wear Cove, and Miller Cove are especially good. Open fields near woodland edges are among the best singing locations. Songs are given from dusk to dawn, especially on moonlit nights with little wind, from April into June. The peaks of singing are dusk and dawn. There are no really good places where one can be sure of finding this bird in the park, but it has been recorded at Cades Cove, Sugarlands, and Gatlinburg.

◆**Whip-poor-will**—A fairly common summer resident in the park, it begins its nocturnal singing about half an hour after sunset and often continues until dawn. It is most vocal early in the nesting season and on still moonlit nights. Songs begin soon after the bird arrives in late March and may be heard into late September. Listen for this species below 3,000 feet in many locations including Cosby, Cherokee Orchard, Cataloochee, Cades Cove, Elkmont, Tremont, and Deep Creek. Recently, a good area to see and hear this bird has been along the back road between Metcalf Bottoms Picnic Area and Wear Cove.

◆**Common Nighthawk**—This is a fairly common migrant with large flocks seen in August and September as they head southward during the day. It is harder to find as a summer resident in the park where it is present by the third week of April. Cades Cove is the best place to look and listen within park boundaries, but your chances will improve if you seek the bird in the nearby towns of Cherokee, Bryson City, Townsend, Pigeon Forge, and Gatlinburg. In towns, it nests on flat-topped buildings and feeds on the wing under the street lights.

◆**Songbirds**—At least three species of songbirds, the Northern Mockingbird, Yellow-breasted Chat, and the Field Sparrow sing frequently enough at night that they should be listed here. Moonlit nights are best if you are staying in one of the nearby towns. The Northern Mockingbird uses the artificial street lighting to illuminate his mimicry that may last most of the night, every night, throughout spring and summer.

BIRDS OF THE SHORT SELF-GUIDING NATURE TRAILS.
There are several self-guiding nature trails of less than a mile in length to be found throughout the park. Each trail is well marked and booklets are available which explain points of interest. You will see many more birds in season than the few species listed, but an effort has been made to point out the most common or conspicuous birds. Your chances will be significantly improved if you know their songs and calls. But, even if you don't know a Northern

Cardinal's song from a Wild Turkey's gobble, you will see many birds if you move along slowly and quietly and remain alert to the movements and sounds around you.

◆**Balsam Mountain**—An easy ¾ mile trail in the mile-high spruce-fir forest starting at Balsam Mountain Campground. Permanent residents include Hairy Woodpecker, Red-breasted Nuthatch, Black-capped Chickadee, Brown Creeper, the erratic Red Crossbill and Cedar Waxwing, American Robin, and Golden-crowned Kinglet. Common Ravens and American Crows fly over and sometimes frequent the nearby campground. Barred Owls, and occasionally the rarer Northern Saw-whet Owl, call at night. The Dark-eyed Junco is the most common species at any time of year. In summer, add Blue-headed Vireo, Veery, Black-throated Green Warbler, Black-throated Blue Warbler, Chestnut-sided Warbler (in the disturbed areas), Canada Warbler, Blackburnian Warbler, and Winter Wren as well as the occasional Gray Catbird, Eastern Towhee, and Chimney Swift.

◆**Cosby**—A one-mile loop beginning at the campground amphitheater. Winter visitors include Dark-eyed Junco, Hermit Thrush, Purple Finch, Fox Sparrow, Brown Creeper, Golden-crowned Kinglet. Yellow-rumped (Myrtle) Warbler, Red-breasted Nuthatch (in conifers), and White-throated Sparrow. Permanent residents include Eastern Screech-Owl, Barred Owl, American Crow, Blue Jay, Northern Cardinal, Carolina Chickadee, Tufted Titmouse, Carolina Wren, White-breasted Nuthatch, Red-bellied Woodpecker, and Ruffed Grouse. In summer add the Chimney Swift, Broad-winged Hawk, Summer Tanager, Louisiana Water-thrush near streams, Acadian Flycatcher, Whip-poor-will, Wood Thrush, Red-eyed Vireo, American Redstart, Worm-eating Warbler, Kentucky Warbler, Black-and-white Warbler, Northern Parula warbler, Black-throated Green Warbler, and in the campground, Chipping Sparrow.

◆**Cove Hardwood**—A ¾ mile loop starting near the entrance to the Chimneys Picnic Area. Permanent residents include Downy

Woodpecker, Red-bellied Woodpecker, American Robin, Blue Jay, Carolina Wren, Carolina Chickadee, Tufted Titmouse, Northern Cardinal, Dark-eyed Junco, Eastern Screech-owl, Ruffed Grouse, White-breasted Nuthatch, and Eastern Towhee. Winter visitors include Brown Creeper, Purple Finch, Golden-crowned Kinglet, Yellow-rumped (Myrtle) Warbler, Hermit Thrush, and Yellow-bellied Sapsucker. In summer add Scarlet Tanager, American Redstart, Blue-gray Gnatcatcher, Black-throated Blue Warbler, Black-throated Green Warbler, Blue-headed Vireo, Red-eyed Vireo, Wood Thrush, Eastern Wood-pewee, Acadian Flycatcher, and Great Crested Flycatcher

◆**Elkmont**—A ¾ mile trail starting from the parking area opposite Elkmont Campground. Permanent species include Ruffed Grouse, Eastern Screech-Owl, Pileated Woodpecker, Red-bellied Woodpecker, Carolina Chickadee, Tufted Titmouse, Carolina Wren, White-breasted Nuthatch, American Robin, Blue Jay, Northern Cardinal, and Eastern Towhee. Winter visitors include Dark-eyed Junco, Yellow-bellied Sapsucker, Brown Creeper, Golden-crowned Kinglet, Fox Sparrow, Purple Finch, White-throated Sparrow, and Yellow-rumped (Myrtle) Warbler. In summer add Whip-poor-will, Summer Tanager, Acadian Flycatcher, Yellow-billed Cuckoo, Red-eyed Vireo. Black-and-white Warbler, Ovenbird, Kentucky Warbler, Worm-eating Warbler, Hooded Warbler, Black-throated Green Warbler, Gray Catbird, and Blue-gray Gnatcatcher.

◆**Cades Cove**—A ½ mile trail starting from the Cades Cove Loop Road. Permanent residents include Downy Woodpecker, Northern Cardinal, Carolina Wren, Tufted Titmouse, Carolina Chickadee, Eastern Towhee, Blue Jay, American Crow and Turkey Vulture. Winter visitors include Yellow-rumped (Myrtle) Warbler, Dark-eyed Junco, Hermit Thrush, Fox Sparrow, and Golden-crowned Kinglet. In summer add Summer Tanager, Kentucky Warbler, Hooded Warbler, Ovenbird, Great Crested Flycatcher, Blue-gray Gnatcatcher, and Wood Thrush.

◆**Smokemont**—A short trail near the Oconaluftee River at Smokemont Campground. Permanent residents include Eastern Screech-Owl, Eastern Phoebe, Downy Woodpecker, Red-bellied Woodpecker, Tufted Titmouse, Carolina Chickadee, White-breasted Nuthatch, Carolina Wren, American Robin, Northern Cardinal, Blue Jay, American Crow, Eastern Towhee, Song Sparrow, and Belted Kingfisher (along the river). Winter visitors include Golden-crowned Kinglet, Yellow-rumped (Myrtle) Warbler, Yellow-bellied Sapsucker, Hermit Thrush, Purple Finch, Red-breasted Nuthatch, and White-throated Sparrow. In summer add Louisiana Waterthrush along the river, American Redstart, Hooded Warbler, Ovenbird, Blue-gray Gnatcatcher, Red-eyed Vireo, Acadian Flycatcher, Worm-eating Warbler, Black-throated Green Warbler, Northern Parula warbler, Black-and-white Warbler, Gray Catbird, and Indigo Bunting along the woodland edges.

◆**Spruce-Fir Nature Trail**—A trail in the Canadian zone forest over a mile high and about one mile long. The trailhead is on the Clingmans Dome Road, about four miles from Newfound Gap. Permanent residents include Common Raven, Hairy Woodpecker, Black-capped Chickadee, Red-breasted Nuthatch, Barred Owl, the erratic Pine Siskin and Red Crossbill, Brown Creeper, Golden-crowned Kinglet, American Robin, and the abundant Dark-eyed Junco. Winter visitors include White-winged Crossbill (rare) and Evening Grosbeak. In summer add Olive-sided Flycatcher, Winter Wren, Northern Saw-whet Owl, Chestnut-sided Warbler (in disturbed areas), Black-throated Blue Warbler, Black-throated Green Warbler, Canada Warbler, Blackburnian Warbler, Blue-headed Vireo, and Veery.

◆**Sugarlands**—About a mile walk starting from the paved trail near the visitor center. Permanent residents include Eastern Phoebe (near the stream), Pileated and Downy Woodpeckers, Northern Cardinal, Eastern Towhee, Carolina Wren, Tufted Titmouse, Carolina Chickadee, American Robin, American Goldfinch (around the parking lot), Eastern Screech-Owl, Blue Jay, and Song Sparrow (near the visitor center). Winter visitors include Evening Grosbeak, Purple Finch, Pine Siskin (erratic), Dark-eyed Junco, Yellow-rumped (Myrtle) Warbler. Yellow-bellied Sapsucker, Hermit Thrush, and White-throated Sparrow; in summer add Scarlet and Summer tanagers, Northern Parula warbler, Black-and-white Warbler, Blue-gray Gnatcatcher, Red-eyed and Yellow-throated vireos, Worm-eating Warbler, Black-throated Green Warbler, Gray Catbird, Northern Rough-winged and Barn swallows (over the visitor center), Kentucky Warbler, Hooded Warbler, Indigo Bunting and Yellow Warbler (around the parking area), Yellow-throated Warbler, Golden-winged Warbler (uncommon), Chipping Sparrow (near the visitor center), Louisiana Waterthrush, Wood Thrush, Brown-headed Cowbird, Common Grackle, and Eastern Meadowlark (on the lawn).

◆**Roaring Fork Motor Nature Trail**—This five-mile self-guiding motor route starts from Cherokee Orchard, four miles south of Gatlinburg via Airport Road. It's a one-way road that is steep and winding (no trailers or motorhomes) with a few turnouts from which you can bird. Permanent residents include Eastern Screech-Owl, Barred Owl, Pileated Woodpecker, Downy Woodpecker, Blue Jay, Carolina Chickadee, Tufted Titmouse, Carolina Wren, White-breasted Nuthatch, American Robin, Golden-crowned Kinglet (in hemlocks), Northern Cardinal, Eastern Towhee, and Dark-eyed Junco (in highest part of loop). Winter visitors include Hermit Thrush, Yellow-bellied Sapsucker, Red-breasted Nuthatch, Yellow-rumped (Myrtle) Warbler, Purple Finch, Fox Sparrow, and White-throated Sparrow. In summer add Whip-poor-will, Yellow-billed Cuckoo, Great Crested Flycatcher, Broad-winged Hawk, Ruby-throated Hummingbird, Chimney Swift (overhead), Gray Catbird, Blue-gray Gnatcatcher, Wood Thrush, Red-eyed Vireo, Yellow-throated Vireo, Blue-headed Vireo, Black-and-white Warbler, Ovenbird, Black-throated Green Warbler, Black-throated Blue Warbler, Blackburnian Warbler (in hemlocks), Northern Parula warbler, Scarlet Tanager, Summer Tanager, and Rose-breasted Grosbeak. Also see the information on Cherokee Orchard in the earlier section "Birding from the Lowlands to 'Canada.'"

PHOTOGRAPHING BIRDS

The challenge of photographing birds has given me countless hours of pleasure over the past twenty years. Birds are active animals, often with brilliant plumages that make rewarding subjects for photography. Because of their small size, wariness, and habits of perching in the treetops, photographing birds requires both skill and luck.

The basic equipment required is a single lens reflex camera (most 35mm cameras) and one or more telephoto lenses. Because most birds are small and don't allow a close approach, it is best to have a telephoto lens with a minimum focal length of at least 300mm.

Birds are often not in full sunlight, so faster films with an ASA (DIN) of 200 or greater are recommended for field work. I have seen many acceptable shots made with handheld cameras, even some with long telephoto lenses attached, however, for increased sharpness I recommend you use a sturdy tripod whenever possible.

Much of my field photography is conducted in a photoblind (or hide as the English call them). A blind is anything that can conceal you from the wildlife. Your automobile can serve as an excellent photoblind, allowing a close approach to wild animals as long as you stay inside. Add a window mount for your camera and turn off the engine before you snap the picture and you have a steady platform that you can get many good shots from. My favorite blinds are canvas or cloth tent-like coverings draped over a frame designed to support it. The covering is usually made of earthtone colors that blend in with the natural landscape. Working from such a blind on the ground or from a platform on a tower allows you to photograph birds from only a few feet away. I often use strobe lighting when photographing nesting birds from my blind, but fast lenses and fast film will also allow you to use natural lighting effectively. Striking close-ups can be obtained by using a combination of a blind and telephoto lenses.

BIRD SONGS
Learning through Mnemonics

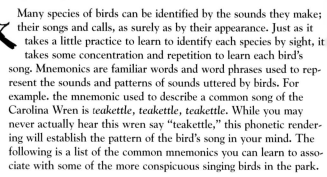

Many species of birds can be identified by the sounds they make; their songs and calls, as surely as by their appearance. Just as it takes a little practice to learn to identify each species by sight, it takes some concentration and repetition to learn each bird's song. Mnemonics are familiar words and word phrases used to represent the sounds and patterns of sounds uttered by birds. For example. the mnemonic used to describe a common song of the Carolina Wren is *teakettle, teakettle, teakettle*. While you may never actually hear this wren say "teakettle," this phonetic rendering will establish the pattern of the bird's song in your mind. The following is a list of the common mnemonics you can learn to associate with some of the more conspicuous singing birds in the park.

Broad-winged Hawk: a high-pitched, whistled *pee-weeeee*.

Northern Bobwhite: the bird whistles its name, *bobwhite*.

Barred Owl: a hooted *Who cooks for you—who cooks for youall?*

Whip-poor-will: whistles its name, *whip-poor-will, whip-poor-will*.

Great Crested Flycatcher: a loud whistled *wheep or creeep*.

Eastern Phoebe: the bird says its name with a husky *fee-be, fee-be*.

Eastern Wood-Pewee: a plaintive whistled *pee-oh-wee, pee-err*.

Acadian Flycatcher: a short, explosive sneeze, *peet-sa* or *pee-up*.

Blue Jay: a loud raucous *thief, thief, thief* or *jay, jay, jay*.

Black-capped Chickadee: a whistled *fee-bee* or *fee-bee-ee* (two or three notes); calls *Chick-aa-dee-dee-dee-dee* (similar to the Carolina Chickadee).

Carolina Chickadee: a whistled *fee-bee, fee-bu* (four notes).

Tufted Titmouse: a whistled *peter, peter, peter*.

White-breasted Nuthatch: a nasal *yank, yank, yank.*

Carolina Wren: a loud *teakettle, teakettle, teakettle.*

Blue-gray Gnatcatcher: a thin lispy *spee, spee, spee.*

White-eyed Vireo: a rapid *quick-with-the-beer-check.*

Blue-headed, Red-eyed, and Yellow-throated vireos: a steadily delivered song that rises and falls made up of notes separated by pauses; *look up . . . , see me? . . . , over here . . . , higher . . .* and so on.

Yellow Warbler: a whistled *sweet, sweet, sweet, I'm so sweet.*

Chestnut-sided Warbler; *please, please, pleased to meetcha.*

Black-throated Blue Warbler: a buzzy *I am laz-zzzy.*

Black-throated Green Warbler: a high pitched whistled *zee, zee, zee, zoo, za* or *zay, zay, zay, zoo, zee.*

Black-and-white Warbler: like a high pitched squeaking wheel, *wee-see, wee-see, wee-see, wee-see.*

Ovenbird: rising with each note higher and more emphatic than the last, *teach, teach, teach, TEACH.*

Kentucky Warbler: a loud *tur-dle, tur-dle, tur-dle* or *churree, churree, churree, churree.*

Common Yellowthroat: *witchy, witchy, witchy, witch.*

Hooded Warbler: a loud *wheeta, wheeta, wheeteeo.*

Scarlet Tanager: *chip-er* (call note).

Northern Cardinal: several loud whistled variations including: *what, cheer, cheer, cheer; cheer, cheer, cheer, whot, whot, whot;* or *birdy, birdy, birdy, birdy.*

Indigo Bunting: a whistled *sweet, sweet, sweeter, sweeter, here, here.*

Eastern Towhee: *drink-your-teeeeeee!*

White-throated Sparrow: *old Sam Peabody, Peabody, Peabody.*

CONTRIBUTORS

FRED J. ALSOP, III is a professor and former chairman of the Department of Biological Sciences at East Tennessee State University. An avid birder and field biologist, he has identified more than 3,200 species of birds in his travels. As a photographer of birds for more than 30 years, his wildlife pictures have appeared in numerous books and magazines. He has published more than 125 articles and notes in national and international journals on birds. For more than 37 years he has birded in Great Smoky Mountains National Park as one of its millions of annual visitors, as a seasonal park naturalist, and as a birding tour leader and instructor. He is author of several regional and national bird books including the Smithsonian Handbooks, *Birds of North America, Eastern and Western Region*. Dr. Alsop has a Ph.D. in zoology from the University of Tennessee at Knoxville.

RAY HARM embarked on a project in 1962 which was the first of its kind since the late nineteenth century: the painting of a complete fine art collection of the wildlife of North America. In 1963, Ray Harm Wildlife Art, Inc., published the first limited edition print of Mr. Harm's work and the limited edition art print industry for wildlife artists was born.

An active conservationist and the founding artist of Frame House Gallery, he has raised significant funds through his lectures and paintings for numerous ecology and conservation institutions. Mr. Harm's original painting of the Northern Parula was created and donated for this book.

G. RONALD AUSTING is an internationally known photographer and videographer of birds whose photos have graced the pages of every major birding magazine and ornithology text for the past 45 years. His video footage of birds has been featured in many television programs on birds and natural history.

BIBLIOGRAPHY &
SELECTED REFERENCES

Alsop, Fred J., III. 1968 (revised 1985). *Birds of the Great Smoky Mountains Field Check List.* Published by Great Smoky Mountains National Park. Gatlinburg, TN.

Alsop, Fred J., III. 1988. *Birds of the Great Smoky Mountains. A Checklist for the Birds of Great Smoky Mountains National Park.* Published by Great Smoky Mountains Association. Gatlinburg, TN.

Gruson, Edward S. 1972. *Words for Birds: A Lexicon of North American Birds with Biographical Notes.* Quadrangle Books, Inc., New York, N.Y. (Author's note: This is a highly recommended guide that includes the origins of the common and scientific names of most North American species of birds. I have often referred to it when I was curious about the etymological history of many of the names of our familiar birds.)

Stupka, Arthur. 1963. *Notes on the Birds of Great Smoky Mountains National Park.* The University of Tennessee Press. Knoxville, TN. (Author's note: This work remains the single best source of natural history information on the birds of this national park.)

The Chat. A quarterly journal of the Carolina Bird Club. Permanent address: Shuford Memorial Sanctuary, P.O. Box 1220, Tryon, N.C. 28782. (Author's note: This journal contains many notes on the birds of Great Smoky Mountains National Park.)

The Migrant. A quarterly journal of ornithology first published in June, 1930. Published by the Tennessee Ornithological Society. (Author's note: There are many field records, species accounts and short papers on the birds of Great Smoky Mountains National Park published in this journal.)

INDEX

Blackbird, Red-winged, 129
Bluebird, Eastern, 86
Bobwhite, Northern, 48
Bunting, Indigo, 122

Cardinal, Northern, 120
Catbird, Gray, 91
Chat, Yellow-breasted, 117
Chickadee
    Black-capped, 75, 144-5
    Carolina, 76
Chuck-wills-widow, 155-6
Cowbird, Brown-headed, 132
Creeper, Brown, 80
Crossbill, Red, 141
Crow, American, 73
Cuckoo, Yellow-billed, 51

Dove, Mourning, 50

Falcon, Peregrine, 45
Finch, Purple, 134
Flicker, Northern, 63
Flycatcher
    Acadian, 66
    Great Crested, 68
    Olive-sided, 144

Gnatcatcher, Blue-gray, 85
Goldfinch, American, 136
Grackle, Common, 131
Grosbeak
    Evening, 137
    Rose-breasted, 121

Grouse, Ruffed, 46

Hawk
    Broad-winged, 42
    Red-tailed, 43
    Sharp-shinned, 41
Heron, Green, 38
Hummingbird, Ruby-throated, 57

Jay, Blue, 72
Junco, Dark-eyed, 128

Kestrel, American, 44
Kingbird, Eastern, 69
Kingfisher. Belted, 58
Kinglet
    Golden-crowned, 83
    Ruby-crowned, 84

Meadowlark, Eastern, 130

Nighthawk, Common, 156
Nuthatch
    Red-breasted, 78
    White-breasted, 79

Oriole, Orchard, 133
Ovenbird, 111
Owl
    Barred, 53, 155
    Eastern Screech, 52, 154
    Great Horned, 154-5
    Northern Saw-whet, 54, 138-9

rula, Northern, 99
noebe, Eastern, 67
ven, Common, 74, 142
edstart, American, 109
obin, American, 90

psucker, Yellow-bellied, 60
skin, Pine, 135
parrow
  Chipping, 124
  Field, 125
  Song, 126
  White-throated, 127
arling, European, 94
vallow
  Barn, 71
  Northern Rough-winged, 70
ift, Chimney, 56

nager
  Scarlet, 119
  Summer, 118
rasher, Brown, 92
rush
  Swainson's, 88
  Wood, 89
tmouse, Tufted, 77
whee, Eastern, 123
rkey, Wild, 47, 141-2

ery, 87
reo
  Blue-headed, 96
  Red-eyed, 98
  White-eyed, 95
  Yellow-throated, 97

Vulture
  Black, 39
  Turkey, 40

Warbler
  Black-and-white, 108
  Black-throated Blue, 102, 146
  Black-throated Green, 104
  Blackburnian, 105
  Canada, 116, 145
  Chestnut-sided, 101
  Hooded, 115
  Kentucky, 113, 143
  Palm, 107
  Swainson's, 139
  Worm-eating, 110, 143-4
  Yellow, 100
  Yellow-rumped, 103
  Yellow-throated, 106

Waterthrush, Louisiana, 112
Waxwing, Cedar, 93
Whip-poor-will, 55, 156
Wood-Pewee, Eastern, 65
Woodcock, American, 49, 153-4
Woodpecker
  Downy, 61
  Hairy, 62
  Pileated, 64, 142
  Red-bellied, 59
Wren
  Carolina, 81
  Winter, 82

Yellowthroat, Common, 114